A Short History of Painting   From Cave Art to Jackson Pollock

Florens Deuchler

A Short History of Painting

From Cave Art to Jackson Pollock

HARRY N. ABRAMS, INC., Publishers, NEW YORK

Library of Congress Catalog Card Number: 68–18128
Copyright 1968 in Switzerland by Kunstkreis, Lucerne
All rights reserved. No part of the contents of this book
may be reproduced without the written permission of the
publishers HARRY N. ABRAMS, INCORPORATED,
NEW YORK, N.Y.
Printed in Switzerland by Mengis & Sticher, Lucerne
Bound in the Netherlands
Reproduction rights reserved by S.P.A.D.E.M., Paris, and
Cosmopress, Geneva, where relevant

Contents

Introduction

Painting is the clearest and most accurate mirror of a given period. No other visual art provides us with such reliable information about how a people, a generation, or an individual saw the world. To a greater degree than sculpture or architecture, painting explores, masters, and shapes the world around us. In this medium of color the painter perpetuates his impressions of outer and inner reality: human and nonhuman nature, abstract ideas, and religious symbols; whatever he sees, remembers, or invents. He sets down his vision on a flat surface and passes it on to contemporaries and later generations as a visual record, as his testimony about a specific experience.

Spiritual and artistic creations enter history in many guises, such as written texts, drawings, or reliefs. The painted picture, however, is the most valuable of all such documents because it most visibly perpetuates a particular moment of time, singled out by the artist himself as especially significant.

So long as the painter works with colors and endeavors to reproduce nature's colored image, his work will be naturalistic. The techniques of mixing colors and spreading them over various surfaces vary from generation to generation and from artist to artist. Brushwork is essentially subjective and has an expressive value comparable to handwriting. Since the Renaissance—and to an even greater extent since the Baroque period—a painter's handling of the brush (in conjunction with his compositional methods and preference for certain subjects and colors rather than others) has been an important aspect of his individual style. The art historian draws upon such "graphological" evidence when he assigns works to particular stages of a given artist's development.

Whereas architecture and sculpture create three-dimensional objects—that is, objects that take up space just like elements of the natural environment—painting is limited to a two-dimensional area: a plastered wall, a piece of canvas, a wooden panel, a copper plate, a sheet of paper or parchment.

The most important element of painting is color, which may be applied in many ways: as oil, wax, tempera, watercolor, or pastel. Areas of color may be sharply set off one from another so as to give rise to boundary lines or, as in Impressionist painting, may do without sharp delineation almost entirely.

The art of painting can thus be defined as a method of exploring the world through the medium of color. In landscapes, interiors, still lifes, and portraits the artist can represent what he actually sees. In religious and historical paintings he draws upon his memory and imagination. But he can also take down his subjective visions without objective counterparts, translating them into visible, "legible" records.

In this book we shall deal with two main groups of subjects which have been treated in painting over the centuries. The first is religious art, which in Europe is almost exclusively Christian, and includes primarily the Life and Passion of Christ and the lives of the saints; "prefigurative" scenes from the Old Testament are often introduced. One subject of particular importance is the Madonna and Child. The mother motif is as old as art itself, but after the advent of Christianity it was formulated in important new ways.

The second main group of subjects discloses the bewilderingly rich world of profane or secular imagery: glorification of the secular ruler and his court, his warlike exploits and peacetime achievements, and depictions of everyday life in portraits, interiors, still lifes, animal pictures, and so on.

Every period of painting, as it builds upon the experiences and conquests of preceding generations, has been marked by new discoveries. Secular art has often gone back to religious forms and images, adapting them to its own requirements, "secularizing" them. As a result, the art of the West exhibits remarkable iconographic consistency. Motifs and images have repeatedly been used over generations, even over centuries, and in this way the formal unity of Western art has prevailed over mere stylistic changes. In this art, the role of tradition can hardly be overestimated. Even when there appear to be gaps in continuity, ties with centuries-old pictorial tradition—occasionally going back to antiquity—are never entirely broken. Not until very recently, with the rise of abstract art, has there been a wholly new and unprecedented departure from all that went before. By penetrating into the world of abstract form, art has not lost any of its vitality—on the contrary, it has extraordinarily enriched our picture of the world.

Plate 1. Prehistoric Cave Painting. c. 15,000–10,000 B.C. Lascaux (Dordogne), France

From Prehistoric Times to the Byzantine Era

LASCAUX

The frieze of little horses at Lascaux, in western France (pl. 1), poses a host of problems. The animals and signs are rendered in varying sizes, not subject to a common scale. They move now to the left, now to the right, in different postures and with different kinds of movement, and they overlap one another quite unpredictably. Considering that this prehistoric painting—only a few details are reproduced here—dates from between 15,000 and 10,000 B.C., the artist's intentions can only be a matter of conjecture. He seems to have been interested in differentiating a number of species, and in suggesting great abundance. Also, individual figures were repeated several times in order to suggest a herd, which as such would represent a threat to a lone hunter. Yet it would be a mistake

to interpret the detail shown here as a composition in the modern sense of the word.

To the modern viewer, the animals seem portrayed with surprising realism. Occasionally the contours of the rock face are exploited to give relief to the figures and thus enhance the impression of life. The artists of Lascaux (and also of Altamira and other caves) must have enjoyed a highly developed visual memory to reproduce elements from their environment so exactly.

Prehistoric paintings are for the most part found in the vicinity of subterranean rivers or pot holes and at sites associated with occult forces (the grotto of Lourdes was a prehistoric cave). The caves decorated with paintings were probably places where people gathered for worship and ritual dancing. Dancing, painting, and music—the oldest art forms—were all elements of the ritual, and

Plate 2. Egyptian Tomb Painting. Three Girl Musicians.
c. 1450–1425 B.C. Tomb of Nakht, Thebes

each served to enhance the others. That primitive hunters gathered at such sites to practice various kinds of magic, including fertility magic with representations of pregnant animals, has been abundantly documented by anthropologists.

EGYPT

The oldest Egyptian paintings, dating from the fourth millennium B.C., are in the tradition of the prehistoric cave paintings. Unlike those at Lascaux, however, they are very detailed, occasionally even anecdotal. Men and animals, whether in combat or peaceful co-existence, are represented much like hieroglyphics, with the little figures scattered over the walls. Only occasionally do they form groups which can be interpreted as early attempts at the sequential portrayal of a narrative action.

Our example (pl. 2) is typical of the last phase in the artistic development of the Nile valley: here a pictorial pattern developed in earlier periods has become a cut and dried formula. It also illustrates a pictorial theme which was to be taken up by the Greeks, through whom it eventually reached the whole of the western world. This is the theme of individual figures involved in a common activity. The reproduction shows a detail of the grave decoration from the tomb of Nakht, a priest of Amon and government official under Amenhotep II. Three girls, entertaining at a banquet, are depicted: the first is playing the double flute or oboe, the second a kind of lute, and the third a harp.

This wall painting is far more naturalistic than those at Lascaux. Only the strongly stylized figures of the girls betray the artist's adherence to a long and firmly established tradition. Over many centuries an image of man had been fashioned which met the requirements of the Pharaohs' court ceremonial. This work reflects the life and attitudes of urban officials, not of the majority of the population who toiled in the fields. The refined gestures are treated in strict adherence to a formal canon which is an essential feature of Egyptian art. The heads are shown in profile in order to avoid any distortion or ambiguity; there is mystery in the isolation of the eyes, which are seen frontally; elaborately made up, each eye looks like a precious stone.

The painting is not in perspective. The figures stand at the forward edge of a stagelike space. A few overlappings—though as a rule avoided—suggest that some figures are to be perceived as just back or in front of others. Overlapping limbs (chiefly arms) serve as a sophisticated device for creating a rhythmic group, making the individual figures elements of a subtle garlandlike harmony of lines.

Plate 3. Proto-Argive Vase. The Blinding of Polyphemus. c. 675 B.C. Museum, Argos, Greece

Plate 4. Attic Black-figured Amphora. Hercules and the Erymanthian Boar. c. 525 B.C. British Museum, London

GREECE

Portrayals of dramatically intensified action were not alien to the ceremonious art of Egypt, but its battle scenes and similar subjects strike the modern viewer as overstylized, almost like ballets: the horror and agony of death simply are not conveyed.

The Greeks and Cretans were much more naturalistic than the Egyptians, as is shown even by the earliest of their paintings which have come down to us—all but a few of them vase paintings. The Greeks do not shrink from representing pain. On the contrary, they depict a hunted, frightened, dying animal—as well as the most gruesome incidents from their mythology—in close detail. The *Iliad* and the *Odyssey* provided them with an inexhaustible store of motifs. The fragment from a proto-Argive vase reproduced here (pl. 3) dating from the seventh century B.C. illustrates an episode from the *Odyssey*. Aided by his companions, Odysseus is putting out the single eye of the cyclops Polyphemus by driving a stake through it. The giant has been taken by surprise; the blood is pouring down his cheek and beard.

In this example dating from the early geometric period we find an element that was eventually to take on great importance in the formal organization of paintings: the frame. This scene is set off from

the other vase decoration around it, so that in itself it makes a *pinax* (picture). Time and again we find such "framed" scenes in Greek vase painting, though other methods of decoration were employed as well.

An Attic amphora (pl. 4) from the golden age of the black-figured style is decorated with an episode from the life of Hercules. The hero is shown hurling the Erymanthian boar at his enemy Eurystheus, who is hiding inside a vessel. A figure on the left is holding the hero's club. On the right, the goddess Athena (supposed to be invisible) ensures the success of the exploit. The area covered by the picture stands out as a bright surface on the body of the black vase. Note how skillfully the Greeks composed such pictures to fit a curved surface. From the early Dipylon pottery onward, Greek vase decoration, whether figurative or abstract, was adapted to the form of the vessel, following, interpreting, and accentuating the swellings and hollows of the surface.

Little has come down to us about the use of color in Greek monumental painting. On the many surviving examples of vase painting (apart from the Lekythos vases, which have a white ground), we find black, red-brown, and more rarely white; the vigor and beauty derive mainly from the vivacity of line. The figures always strike us as drawings rather than paintings. This art reached its first

Plate 5. Kleophrades Painter. Red-figured painting of a Maenad from a pointed amphora. c. 510 B.C. Staatliche Antikensammlungen, Munich

Plate 6. Etruscan Tomb Painting. Flute Player. c. 480 B.C. Tomb of the Leopards, Tarquinia

high point late in the sixth century B.C., shortly before the black-figured style gave way to the red-figured style.

The detail of a Maenad by the Kleophrades Painter (c. 510 B.C.) here shown in enlargement (pl. 5) testifies to the excellence of Greek vase painting and the economy of the means employed. The contrasts between light and dark areas, like those between the thin and the thicker lines (rendering the textures of the various garments) are delicately balanced. The parallel and the wavy lines are also handled with great mastery. The virtuoso shorthand which here renders eye, nose, mouth, and eyebrow has been revived in our own day by Picasso.

ETRURIA AND ROME

Contemporaries of the Greek vase painters, especially the Etruscans, were deeply impressed by their work: by their "classical" formulation of the human figure, the beautiful lines of the garments, and the vivacity of its movements. They accepted the guidance of Athens—the "Paris of antiquity"—in matters concerning the arts, and strove to copy the Hellenes as faithfully as possible. The finest Etruscan paintings have been found in tombs

alongside some of the very finest Greek vases. The most important Etruscan cemeteries are in central Italy, mainly near Tarquinia. The Etruscan *Flute Player* (pl. 6), painted about 480 B.C., is a detail from the Tomb of the Leopards. Next to its Greek originals this Italic musician is a bit awkward. The proportions are wrong: the hands too large, the head too small, the legs too long, and the feet too big. Nevertheless, the bucolic intensity and the cheerful liveliness of the figure are unforgettable. Since so few examples of Etruscan art have come down to us, it is impossible to say with certainty whether these "deformations" were deliberate stylizations or the result of provincial awkwardness. If they were deliberate, what we have here was an attempt to break away from the Greek ideal of beauty in the direction of greater expressiveness.

Ancient Italy, the southern portion of which had been colonized by the Greeks, played a very important role in the history of European art. In addition to Etruscan painting and sculpture it gave rise to Roman art, which has been more widely influential. We shall discuss here only one branch of the latter —wall painting. The most important examples were found at Pompeii, Herculaneum, Boscoreale, and Primaporta. At Pompeii we can view Roman painting in a broad context. The painted decorations of the House of the Vetii (pl. 7) date from A.D. 63 to 79, just prior to the destruction of

12

Plate 7. Pompeian Wall Painting. Decoration of a room in the House of the Vetii, Pompeii. A.D. 63–79

Pompeii by the eruption of Mount Vesuvius in A.D. 79. It must be kept in mind that this relatively late work was preceded by a long development, and that it reflects various traditions. The main reason, however, for including it in our survey is that it represents a type of wall decoration which was imitated for many centuries to come.

Above a socle which is subdivided by panels rises a wall articulated by slender little columns supporting richly carved beams. Actually the columns and beams, with the shadows they cast as well, are painted on the wall in *trompe-l'œil*. The illusion is carried further than this, however. Fantastic architectural elements in the corners of the room seem to be "outside" the house, views through corner "windows." Painted in intricate perspective, they make the interior space appear larger than it is. On a panel nearer the middle of the room we see what seems to be a picture hanging on the wall, but this too is a visual illusion: it is painted directly on the wall. It shows the infant Hercules strangling the snakes coiled around him, to the astonished horror of his parents and nurse. The eagle of Jupiter watches over the scene. The picture is presumably a copy of a Greek painting done in the fourth or third century B.C. We came across the framed picture earlier in Greek art (see pl. 3). In Pompeii we see how much further the innovation was carried and how skillfully and dramatically

the action was organized within an arbitrary rectangular space. Note how the expressive gestures of the figures resemble those of actors on a stage. The adjacent views in architectural perspective give an illusion of opening-out space that perfectly balances the strong framing elements around the picture.

FAYUM

Just as Pompeian wall paintings and Roman mosaics go back to Greek originals, the portraits on mummies found in the Fayum in Lower Egypt (pl. 8) reflect the tradition of Greek portrait painting. Few Greek portraits have come down to us, and it is only from works which derive from them and from references found in ancient literary sources that we can imagine what they were like.

About six hundred of these mummy portraits have so far been uncovered. Painted on wood in wax colors, they mostly date from Roman times, from between the first and the third centuries of our era. These portraits seem to have taken the place of the masks we find in Egyptian tombs of more ancient date, and were actually fastened to the head of the mummified corpse. The faces are always in frontal view, and each evokes strikingly individual char-

13

Plate 8. Egyptian Mummy Portrait from the Fayum.
c. A.D. 200–250. Liebighaus, Frankfort

acteristics. To the historian the Fayum portraits are especially interesting because they give us glimpses of the technique that was used here, involving several layers of color, with white highlights and dark flesh tones intended to enhance the plastic effect.

EARLY CHRISTIAN ART

Among the earliest examples of Christian art in Europe are the paintings in the Roman catacombs. They refer symbolically to the life and teachings of Christ, the Cross serving as sign of universal redemption. The term actually used by the early Christians for these mazelike underground burial places was *coemeterium*. The word "catacomb" derives from *coemeterium ad catacumbas* (the name given to the tomb of Saint Sebastian near Rome). In addition to the leading motif of the Cross—the symbol of the new faith—there are other symbols. These include the fish, the dove, the vine, flowers and trees (to represent the Garden of Eden), the lamb, and Jesus portrayed as the Good Shepherd. The last is sometimes a handsome youth reminiscent of Apollo or Orpheus, at other times a venerable teacher in the manner of ancient philosophers.

The new Christian imagery did not "surface," so to speak, until the fourth century A.D., after the Christian faith was officially recognized by the Edict of Milan (313) and proclaimed the state religion (the pagan temples were closed in 391). From this point on this specifically Christian imagery becomes more and more widely and prominently displayed, especially in the churches. Christian iconography was developed very gradually out of motifs and forms that had long flourished around the shores of the Mediterranean, at the same time that Christianity was developing out of a number of pagan religions, only very gradually asserting features unmistakably its own.

The great cycles of pictures painted on the walls of the basilicas served edifying and didactic purposes. They told the Christian story to those who could not read, "illustrating" episodes from the Old and the New Testaments and from Church history. Whereas the early Christian paintings in the catacombs repeat a few motifs over and over again—Noah's Ark, Daniel in the Lions' Den, for example—the later frescoes, mosaics, and illuminations introduce entirely new modes of expression. They are the first cycles of narrative painting in European art, and they stimulated a development that was to continue for centuries.

The earliest such narrative sequences were executed in tiny colored stones. Mosaics were part of the

Plate 9. Ravenna Mosaic. The Miraculous Draught of Fishes (The Calling of Saints Peter and Andrew). c. 526. Sant'Apollinare Nuovo, Ravenna

heritage of late antique splendor, a more lasting variant of precious but perishable tapestry. Perhaps the most famous of the Roman mosaics is *The Battle of Issus,* discovered in the House of the Faun in Pompeii (now in the National Museum, Naples). The delicate configurations of colored stones in this mosaic imitate brushstrokes, and it seems certain that this mosaic was a copy of a Hellenistic painting. Only a few small mosaics have come down to us with the early Christian art preserved in the Roman catacombs. They follow Greco-Roman tradition, but the representations are very much simplified and no longer give the illusion of painted pictures. The religious character of these mosaics is only apparent in a relatively few repeated symbols and motifs. The first large Christian mosaic (c. 400) is in the apse of the church of Santa Pudenziana in Rome. It represents Christ enthroned, surrounded by the apostles. One of the most splendid early Christian mosaic sequences, in Santa Maria Maggiore, was executed during the reign of Pope Sixtus III (432–440). Scenes from the youth of the Redeemer and from the Old Testament can still be seen on the triumphal arch above the choir and on the walls of the nave. While these mosaics have suffered from the passage of time, and their original aspect has been altered by extensive restorations, they are among the most impressive early Christian works.

The art of mosaic reached perfection in the sixth century of our era—not in Rome, but in Ravenna. The mosaics in the church of Sant'Apollinare Nuovo, which was begun during the reign of Theodoric, make a particularly fine set. They are arranged in three rows along the walls of the nave. *The Miraculous Draught of Fishes* (pl. 9) is one of twenty-six rectangular panels illustrating episodes from the New Testament. The figure of the Redeemer stretches the full height of the picture. Because his disciple and the two fishermen are the objects of his action, they are represented in smaller dimensions; thus the relative importance of the figures is immediately evident to the viewer. This proportional device, in one form or another, was used throughout the Middle Ages. The miracle with which Christ rouses the interest of the fishermen and reveals himself to his future apostles has already taken place: the net is filled. A very few gestures suffice to make the whole episode clear to the viewer.

BYZANTIUM

After the division of the Roman Empire in 395, two capitals—Rome and Constantinople—began to vie for supremacy. Gradually the influence of

Plate 10. Byzantine Manuscript Painting. David Composing the Psalms, illustration from the Paris Psalter. c. 900.
Bibliothèque Nationale, Paris

Plate 11. Byzantine Manuscript Painting. Moses Leading the Israelites through the Red Sea. c. 1100–1125. Topkapi Saray Museum, Istanbul

Constantinople, the eastern capital, made itself felt in the west. It was so strong at times that we can speak of recurrent "waves" of Byzantine influence, reflected in the minor arts, such as manuscript painting, no less than in monumental sculpture, wall painting, and stained glass.

A psalter dating from the so-called Byzantine Renaissance of the tenth century is illustrated with large miniatures in which Greco-Roman forms and motifs are adapted to Christian requirements. Examples of this kind inspired many important works in Sicily, Italy, and the countries north of the Alps. On the back of the first leaf David, the author of the Psalms, is represented with his harp (pl. 10). Behind him, with one hand on his shoulder, is the muse who inspires him and whom letters (to her left) identify as "Melodia." At the bottom we see, on the banks of a small river, David's flock of sheep guarded by a fierce-looking dog. Echo is peeking out from her hiding place. The figure at the lower right personifies the mountains that rise just behind him. In the upper left corner the town of Bethlehem is rendered with a few bold lines in the illusionistic style of Hellenistic painting.

The miniature reproduced here (pl. 11) dates from the beginning of the twelfth century. It comes from one of the many illuminated manuscript sequences produced in Constantinople at that time, a 570-page Octateuch, a volume containing the first eight books of the Old Testament. The illustrated narrative sequence includes no fewer than 352 miniatures and 70 smaller illustrations placed close to the corresponding passages in the text. Our reproduction shows the passage of the Israelites through the Red Sea: "And the LORD went before them by day in a pillar of a cloud, to lead them the way; and by night in a pillar of fire, to give them light" (Exodus 13:21). The bluish-gray figure near the top edge of the picture is a personification of Night in the manner of classical antiquity, indicating that the episode is taking place in darkness: Night obscures the light of Day with a cloak. The pillar of fire is shown at the extreme right. Moses and his people have passed through the Red Sea. Their pursuers with all their men and chariots are drowning as the parted waters rush back together. The leading actors of the drama, Moses and Pharaoh, are distinguished by halos. As for the bizarre mountain formations, we will meet them again in the work of late thirteenth- and fourteenth-century Italian painters (see pl. 17); they survived as part of the Byzantine heritage that later Italian painters called *maniera greca,* or Greek style, accurately identifying the ultimate Greek origin of the Byzantine style.

Plate 12. Romanesque Wall Painting. The Martyrdom of Saints Savinus and Cyprianus. c. 1125–50. Crypt of the Church of Saint-Savin-sur-Gartempe, France

Romanesque Wall Painting

In the early Middle Ages (the Carolingian, Ottonian, and Romanesque periods) churches were decorated with paintings and sculptures. Episodes from the Bible appear on sculptured porches, on tapestries hung along the nave and in the choir, and in frescoes and stained-glass windows. The large areas of wall space provided by Romanesque architecture were especially suited to narrative cycles of wall paintings.

The region of Poitou in western France is famous for its art treasures, especially for its medieval wall paintings. The long barrel vaults presented ideal opportunities for fresco decorations. In connection with the great number of pictures painted, we must remember that in the Middle Ages only members of the clergy could read—ordinary people only learned about the events in the Bible from sermons or from painted and sculptured

representations. The visual narratives supplied especially vivid assistance in grasping the Gospel story.

Before proceeding to discuss examples of medieval painting we should note the conditions under which medieval artists worked, for the character of their art was largely determined by these conditions. What they were we can infer from a few surviving books of patterns, sketchbooks, and similar sources.

Down to the time of Dante (1265–1321) the ideas expressed in painted panels, mosaics, wood and stone sculptures, stained-glass windows, and manuscript illuminations are not so much determined by the individual artists as by tradition. As the external forms, however, depend at least partly on the properties of the medium, the works are not totally devoid of individual expression. Forms and techniques were handed down from teacher to pupil and from artist to artist, often across considerable geographical distances, from the Byzantine east to the countries of the West. Only insofar as style is determined by execution can we speak of a style personal to a given artist. The pictorial tradition, for its part, is the result of a collective artistic effort over many generations. It rarely presents much variation, let alone startling changes. Even during the Renaissance, when a great many motifs became available to artists, the old familiar themes, especially those inspired by the Old and the New Testaments, were slow to be adapted to the new tastes.

During the Middle Ages, then, the pictorial tradition was handed down from one artist to another, and each copied his predecessor as faithfully as he could. Truly original works are rare. Whenever an artist was unable to go and look at the works that had become the accepted models, he would make use of sketchbooks by artists who had. Such books did not contain full or detailed copies in the modern sense, but recorded the typical features of the art as prescribed by tradition. Nor did such books illustrate specific scenes or events. They merely supplied the figurative elements for successive realizations of a traditional motif.

The famous sketchbook of Villard de Honnecourt, a Paris architect, and the Wolfenbüttel pattern book—both dating from the first half of the thirteenth century—strike a new note. Villard's collection of drawings is unique: it contains sketches from nature made by the author in the course of his travels. Along with drawings of the towers of Laon Cathedral and the rose window at Lausanne we find a lion in a cage, and hundreds of other motifs which the artist deemed important enough to record. This method of setting down information goes back thousands of years: tablets showing traditional prototypes for sculpture in relief were prepared for apprentice stonecutters in ancient Egypt. Similar "textbook" models were also used in the Orient and in ancient Greece. For instance, the decorated Attic bowl from Vulci (formerly in Berlin) shows the workshop of a Greek sculptor of the fifth century B.C., including an assortment of molds around a furnace. Little tablets representing various figures are shown hanging on the wall, and were evidently the sculptor's models.

Such practices of the ancient world passed directly into the Middle Ages. Unfortunately the surviving evidence from both periods is scanty. The equipment of the medieval workshops has disappeared without a trace, and the first to be lost were the sketchbooks. They were most vulnerable to destruction because they were in constant use. Not until the time of Albrecht Dürer (1471–1528) and Raphael (1483–1520) were drawings considered to be valuable enough to be preserved for their own sake. The sketchbooks of the Venetian Jacopo Bellini (c. 1400–1470) and the *Housebook* by a contemporary north European master are the first records in which we can follow the successive stages in a work's creation, from first rough sketch to finished picture.

There was no such thing as literary or artistic copyright in the Middle Ages. Artists' opportunities for individual expression were extremely limited; their personalities were completely overshadowed by their works, which were mostly unsigned. Art was pursued for the greater glory of God, a consideration that helped confine it within rules and dogmas. The royal and ecclesiastical patrons who commissioned paintings and sculptures were by no means interested in individual talent: what they expected and got was strict adherence to tradition. Only by following age-old models could the artist be sure to be understood.

The painting in the Church of Saint-Savin-sur-Gartempe reproduced here (pl. 12) shows how the various elements of the scene represented were pieced together in the Romanesque period. This applies not only to the incoherence of the architecture but also to the stereotyped treatment of the figures, taken from a book of models and used in this instance to represent the martyrdom of two saints. A number of other stylistic features also make it possible to assign the frescoes in the crypt and in the barrel vault of the church to the beginning or middle of the twelfth century.

The Stained-Glass Windows of the Gothic Period

Toward the end of the twelfth century Romanesque art gradually loses its severity. A gentler spirit animates figures which begin to move more freely and naturally, and, as it were, to express themselves. Romanesque stiffness disappears entirely with the advent of Gothic art. Now the centuries of struggle to make the Christian faith supreme belong to the past. The Church has proved victorious and dominates the entire life of the community. The new cathedrals are no longer dark and mysterious but full of light and color. What had been broad expanses of wall in the Romanesque churches are now pierced with high arched windows of many-colored stained glass. The foursquare towers give way to graceful spires that seemingly soar to heaven. Indeed, the physical church has become a symbolic image of heaven, the heavenly city of Jerusalem. The high-vaulted ceilings are painted blue, and stars are added to heighten the illusion. As they enter the church the faithful leave the world with all its works behind them and enjoy a foretaste of the kingdom of God.

Gothic art was born in France. The generation which invented it created the finest Gothic cathedrals. Besides book illumination, stained-glass windows represent the finest Gothic achievements. Only in this century have art historians stopped classifying this luminous art under "applied art" or "the crafts." From now on histories of the Gothic period will give a prominent place to stained-glass painting.

Saint Louis (King Louis IX) was the central figure in the spiritual life of France at this time. He was a warrior, a legislator, a Crusader, and a patron of the arts. Construction of the Sainte-Chapelle in Paris (1243–48) is regarded as the culmination of his life's work. All carefully carved stone and exquisite stained glass, the Sainte-Chapelle is truly a "jewel" of a building. It was intended as a shrine to house and protect the Crown of Thorns and other Christian relics recently brought back from the Holy Land. However, the *style Saint Louis* did not influence just architecture, it also shaped the art of stained-glass painting in the new churches. In the same period the art of manuscript illumination enjoyed a magnificent flowering in the royal workshops. The Gothic spirit created a new era.

Western France constitutes a distinct artistic region rich in sculptures, miniatures, and frescoes as well as our finest surviving examples of Romanesque

stained glass. The earliest of the latter is the Le Mans fragment representing the Ascension. Next come the west windows of the cathedral at Poitiers, those at Angers, and finally the famous Madonna of the Trinity at Vendôme. In central and south-eastern France there are important pieces of Romanesque and Gothic stained glass at Bourges, Clermont-Ferrand, and Lyons, but they give no more than a faint suggestion of the era's actual splendor. A third, central group is formed by sequences of stained-glass windows at Saint-Denis and Chartres. In their own way they are as much ahead of their time as the architecture of the churches that house them.

In order to determine the style and interpret the iconography of these works, we must refer briefly to the art of the Meuse valley, which profoundly influenced the art of northern France toward the end of the twelfth century and the beginning of the thirteenth. The finest specimens of Mosan work in France are the Crucifixion in the Church of Saint-Rémy at Reims, and the windows in the choir, including the rose window that dominates them, in the Cathedral of Laon. The design of the latter is superb both architecturally and iconographically. The scenes in the lancet windows combine the early life of Jesus with episodes from the Old Testament which prefigured it. Also celebrated are the Passion, the martyrdom of Saint Stephen (originally planned to constitute a lengthy cycle), and the legend of Theophilus. The rose window is occupied by an enthroned Madonna and Child surrounded by the Prophets (pl. 13), the Apostles, and the twenty-four Elders of the Book of Revelation. Like so many cathedrals in France, that at Laon is dedicated to the Mother of God. This is why her image is placed in the most exalted position: the center of the rose window.

The figure of Saint Marcel in the Collegiate Church of Saint-Quentin (pl. 14) dates from a slightly later period (about 1235). This and some other larger-than-life figures (usually found in the clerestory or upper choir windows) belong to a tradition that goes back at least as far as the Romanesque period. The earliest examples of this tradition in Germany are the windows representing the prophets in the Augsburg cathedral (twelfth century).

The art of glass painting was equally developed in other countries. One of the most important late

Plate 13. Gothic Stained Glass. Old Testament Prophet from the Rose Window in the choir of Laon Cathedral. c. 1210

medieval examples is to be found in the monastery church at Königsfelden, Switzerland.

On May 1, 1308, Albrecht I, a German king and regent of the house of Habsburg, was murdered by his nephew Johann. The crime was perpetrated on the western bank of the Reuss (the king had just crossed to that side of the river). His widow Elisabeth expressed the wish that a monastery bearing the name of Königsfelden be built on the spot where the king had died. As early as 1308–9, two Franciscan monks were conducting services in a newly constructed chapel. In the meantime more land was being purchased and construction had probably started on other buildings. In 1310 the Pope gave his approval, and in 1311 Queen Elisabeth signed documents providing for the erection of a monastery, convent, and church. The church receives light through eleven windows with three lancets each, situated in the choir. The richness of the stained glass is in sharp contrast with the austerity of the interior. Like the rest of the establishment, the windows were gifts of the House of Habsburg. Queen Elisabeth's successor, Queen Agnes, together with the murdered king's sons and grandson, who helped her complete the gigantic building project, appear as donors in the stained-glass windows. From the family records it has been possible to determine that the windows were executed between 1325 and 1330. The choir itself was consecrated in 1330.

The windows form a harmonious iconographic and artistic whole. The narrative sequence begins with the central window on the east side of the choir: the Passion of Christ. The windows to the

Plate 14. Gothic Stained Glass. Saint Marcel. c. 1235. Collegiate Church of Saint-Quentin, France

Plate 15. Gothic Stained Glass. Saint Francis Preaching to the Birds. 1325–30. Abbey Church of Königsfelden, Switzerland

north of it depict the early life of Christ and those to the south the episodes of the Resurrection.

Next to the Apostles shown in the directly adjoining windows are scenes from the lives of Saint Francis and Saint Clare of Assisi. The window devoted to Saint Francis depicts the following episodes: Saint Francis renouncing his heritage, confirmation of the rules of the Franciscan Order by Pope Innocent III, Saint Francis preaching to the birds (pl. 15), the saint receiving the stigmata, and his death. In the window devoted to the life of Saint Clare we see her receiving the blessed palm, her investiture as the head of the Order, her family's attempts to dissuade her from her calling, and the saving of the convent from the Saracens.

Königsfelden played a vital part in introducing perspective elements into the art of stained glass. The gradations and overlapping of colors also contribute to the illusion of space. A similar effect is achieved by representations of movement and posture: reaching forward or backward, sitting, turning away. The new approach, however, is most evident in motifs of Italian origin: sarcophagi, thrones, altars with canopies, friezes, and a number of complicated architectural forms all shown in perspective. These set pieces are placed diagonally, seen either from above or below—occasionally even from one side. But they are not as yet integrated into the pictorial space. Rather, they stand out strongly, for they are not seen from a single point of view and occasionally clash with the rest of the scene.

Precisely where the new development came from is far from certain. The fact that these windows were completed in the remarkably short period of five years suggests that a considerable number of craftsmen were employed, but whether the work was done at Königsfelden or elsewhere is unknown. In any case, only a sizable workshop directed by an outstanding artist could have achieved such brilliant results. Various features of these windows suggest affinities with styles then current in France, the Upper Rhine valley, and Alsace. No preliminary stages, let alone analogies, however, can be followed up in view of the small number of surviving examples. All that is certain is that the Königsfelden style was widely imitated in Alsace. This is proved conclusively by a number of stained-glass windows produced after 1330.

Ricarda Huch has given a poetic account of her impressions on seeing medieval stained glass: "To step into a Gothic church with stained-glass windows is to turn one's back on the world. The new environment is not of this world. The light that comes through stained glass is a transfigured light: *lumen de lumina,* light from a source not itself created. Ancient words evoking eternal mysteries echo in the beholder. Nowhere in nature do our eyes encounter so red a red, so blue a blue—nowhere are colors of such strength so gently harmonized."

The Renaissance in Italy

GIOTTO AND HIS PERIOD

The Italians of the fifteenth and sixteenth centuries used the term "the dark ages" to designate the period between classical antiquity and the Renaissance. The latter term designates a "rebirth" of ancient ideas, modes of feeling, and artistic forms, which can be traced from 1300 onward. Even medieval art of the Romanesque and Gothic periods was felt to be barbaric in comparison with the unsurpassable achievements of antiquity. Not until the nineteenth century were the Middle Ages appreciated and studied for their own sake. Goethe and Schiller began this revision of taste, and although the Romantics went too far in their reaction against long-standing prejudices, eventually a juster and more balanced evaluation of medieval art has been arrived at.

The revival of interest in pre-Christian antiquity went hand in hand with the emergence of new ideas. In Italy, Giotto and his contemporaries began to burst the narrow bounds of medieval tradition with their panel paintings and frescoes, which, with their large format, demanded large surfaces on church walls and brightly lighted palaces. This far-reaching transformation in the artists' expression of the world—evident also in the three-dimensional arts of architecture and sculpture—entailed first of all rejection of the *maniera greca,* the Byzantine style which had dominated the Middle Ages in the entire Mediterranean basin, smothering every spontaneous local or individual expression.

One last surge of Byzantine influence upon Italy must be briefly mentioned because it is closely associated with the beginnings of European easel painting. It provided the initial impulse for the innovations by Tuscan and Umbrian artists of the period just before Giotto, including such masters as Guido da Siena, Duccio di Buoninsegna, and the Roman Pietro Cavallini.

"The great flood of misfortunes, by which poor Italy had been afflicted and overwhelmed, had not only reduced to ruins all buildings of note throughout the land, but what was of far more importance, had caused an utter lack of the very artists themselves. At this time, when the supply seemed entirely exhausted, in the year 1240, by the will of God there was born in the city of Florence, Giovanni surnamed Cimabue, who was to shed the first light in the art of painting." This is how

Plate 16. Tuscan Master. Madonna and Child. c. 1300. Galleria Sabauda, Turin

Giorgio Vasari in his *Lives of the Artists* describes Cimabue's emergence on the historical scene. In 1272 Cimabue was living in Rome, about 1296 he was working at Assisi, and in 1301–2 he created the mosaic representing Saint John (now in a poor state of preservation) in the apse of the cathedral at Pisa. His *Madonna Enthroned,* painted for the church of Santa Trinità in Florence (but now in the Uffizi Gallery), shows that although he began in the *maniera greca* he tried to achieve an ever stronger and more spacious plasticity of design, as well as a monumental solidity of structure.

In the thirteenth century Rome was the leading artistic center. Cimabue and Giotto both studied there. However, after the papal court went into exile in Avignon, northern Italy—especially Florence and Siena—took over the artistic pre-eminence hitherto held by Rome.

Plate 17. Duccio di Buoninsegna. The Temptation of Christ. 1308–11. The Frick Collection, New York

A Tuscan *Madonna and Child* (pl. 16) demonstrates the principles that governed the creations of Italian artists active around 1300. The rigid linear articulation of the picture is Byzantine, and not only contributes to its formal unity but also sums up its spiritual content with uncommon intensity.

One of the first masters to emerge from medieval anonymity was Duccio di Buoninsegna (c. 1260–1318). Slightly older than Giotto, and like him a native of Tuscany, Duccio is looked upon as the first great representative of the Sienese school. Because of his dependence on Byzantine models, he strikes us as a conservative painter, yet his figures exhibit greater freedom and more lifelike features than those in Byzantine paintings.

The Temptation of Christ (pl. 17) originally formed part of Duccio's greatest work, the altar of the cathedral of Siena. It shows how the artist sought to enrich the Biblical scene with details borrowed from the visible world. Admittedly, the treatment of the mountains is highly artificial; set down without relation to one another, their design derives from Byzantine prototypes. The various towns scattered here and there look as though they were created separately on the drawing board, each with its own perspective, before being transferred to the picture. There is no continuity of space between the towns themselves or the towns and the mountains. The gold background further destroys the illusion of space. And yet with his two central

Plate 18. Giotto. The Annunciation to Saint Anne. 1305–6. Arena Chapel, Padua

figures of Christ and the Devil the artist has attempted to suggest depth. Christ stands on a rock, somewhat closer to the viewer than the Devil, whose feet rest lower down on another hill. That so much was attempted at all is a reflection of the new spirit. The two angels, meanwhile, situated beyond the horizon line, are wholly traditional, completely unrelated to the landscape. These figures go back to books of models and embody a design formula more often employed in depictions of the baptism of Christ.

In Italy the transition from classical antiquity to the Middle Ages was especially long and complex. Historians still find it hard to say just when Italian art began. However, the period around 1300 is generally looked upon today as a real turning point. The most important artist of this period was Giotto (c. 1266–1337). He laid the foundations for all later developments. Endowed with a strong individual imagination, he combined the achievements of the immediately preceding generations with memories of the classical past. Giotto mastered all the pictorial means at his disposal, using them to fashion a new image of reality in the same way as his contemporary Dante recast the spoken and written language into a new and powerful instrument. The character of his work was determined in part by the influences of early Christianity and the *maniera greca,* but he also owed something to early medieval art of the north, examples of which

Plate 19. Giotto. The Kiss of Judas. 1305–6. Arena Chapel, Padua

the Lombards and the Goths had brought with them to Italy. No one of these influences was decisive, but all of them enter into Giotto's art as a whole.

The art of Giotto is the earliest specifically Italian art. Such distinctive innovations as intelligible structure, the reality of environing space, modeling in the round, and unity of light, color, and space were not only introduced by Giotto but are also fully present from the outset in his work. For a long time after him they were regarded as obligatory, though in subsequent periods they were adapted to different tastes and conditions. So far as Italian art is concerned the human figure stands

at the center of artistic creation—in this it remains faithful to ancient Mediterranean art. From Giotto on, what the artists will especially call attention to are events significant for their spiritual content.

Giotto's great cycle of frescoes in the upper church of San Francesco at Assisi opens a new chapter in the history of European painting. Together with Cimabue, who decorated the choir and the crossing (i.e., the place where the nave intersects the transept) of the lower church, Giotto directed a large workshop and had a hand in the sequence of episodes from the life of Saint Francis that decorate the walls of the upper church. While historians disagree as to each artist's exact responsibility at

Plate 20. Simone Martini. Christ Bearing the Cross (portion). c. 1340. The Louvre, Paris

Assisi, the decoration of the Arena Chapel in Padua (1305–7) is unmistakably the work of Giotto alone. The frescoes, which were commissioned by Enrico Scrovegni, include scenes from the lives of Christ and Mary, and a splendid *Last Judgment.*

Two of these frescoes, the *Annunciation to Saint Anne* and the *Kiss of Judas,* illustrate essentially different types of composition.

The *Annunciation to Saint Anne* (pl. 18) is set in an interior room. At the left we see a porch with slender piers supporting a balcony and staircase. The main action, however, is depicted behind closed doors. The angel appears at a window to announce to Saint Anne that she will give birth to the Virgin Mary. Saint Anne receives the message alone on her knees, her hands folded in prayer. A serving woman holding a shuttle is curious about what is going on inside the room. Set off by herself on the little porch, the figure of the servant is unforgettable. The anecdote narrated requires no gloss, but other aspects of the picture are unusual. Here the building is rendered in normal perspective, no longer, as in Duccio, purely for its own sake, but to provide a natural space within which the figures are integrated. In contrast to Duccio's *Temptation of Christ,* where narrative action and scenery are merely juxtaposed, here the action is bound up with a given moment of time.

Concentration on one dramatic moment also characterizes the *Kiss of Judas* fresco (pl. 19). The scene involves a great number of figures, mostly soldiers, who merge into an anonymous mass in the background. The protagonists stand out clearly in the center foreground, where Judas is embracing Christ with a theatrical exaggeration, looking Him right in the eye. But is he really in the very center? Look more closely at this picture and you will see that the central action is slightly left of center. The Judas figure actually extends over the center vertical line, as though about to move from the right to the left half of the picture, thus calling attention to his betrayal. On the left we see St. Peter cutting off Malchus' ear. A hooded figure, with his back to the viewer, serves as a kind of screen that keeps us from paying attention to the gruesome incident. In the lower right corner a figure in a violet robe seems to play the role of narrator, wordlessly pointing to the action going on just a little farther back. It is a noisy scene. A horn is being blown, the torches crackle with a good flame, and the sound of clashing arms is heard in the distance.

Simone Martini (1284–1344) worked at first in his native town of Siena. His earliest known work is the *Maestà,* a fresco of the Madonna enthroned with the Holy Child in the Palazzo Pubblico in Siena (1315). One of his late works, *Christ Bearing the Cross* (pl. 20), now in the Louvre, illustrates further developments in the art of painting. In 1340 Simone had joined the papal court at Avignon. Moving to France was of vital importance, not just to him personally, but also for the future

of French painting. What he took to France with him was the ability to represent the human figure in space, which Giotto had first exhibited. His own mature style was enriched with influences from the French painting fashionable at the papal court. The result was a new sub-style characterized by undulating lines and delicate colors. In Simone's work Giotto's dramatic intensity is softened with linear harmonies and lyrical color combinations even in so solemn a work as the one shown here.

The entire art of southern Europe in the Trecento is prefigured here. The same new ideas were picked up and applied by Gentile da Fabriano two generations later.

Simone Martini's *Christ Bearing the Cross* was still being faithfully copied as late as the second decade of the fifteenth century (along with other Italian subjects) in the Chantilly Book of Hours, known as *Les Très Riches Heures du Duc de Berry.*

GENTILE DA FABRIANO

Gentile da Fabriano was born about 1370 and worked in Venice, Brescia, Florence, Siena, Orvieto, and Rome. Still strongly marked by the influence of late Gothic art, his paintings illustrate the Umbrian variant of the "soft" or "international" style practiced at the various courts around 1400. His main work, signed and dated 1423, four years before his death, is the *Adoration of the Magi* in the Uffizi Gallery (pl. 21). In this painting Gentile da Fabriano depicts a swirling movement of many figures, broadening out in the foreground figures of the Magi and coming to rest with the Madonna and Child.

We have already come across other crowd scenes: Giotto's *Kiss of Judas* and Simone Martini's *Christ Bearing the Cross.* But how differently conceived are these three dramatic scenes! In Giotto's work the encounter takes place at the center of the picture—a head-on collision between irresistible forces, which endows the human drama of the betrayal with incomparable vividness. In Simone Martini's work, despite many single motifs, the crowd itself provides the dynamic element. Christ on his way to Golgotha, patiently bearing the cross, moves among sullen and indifferent people. Gentile da Fabriano's subject is the very different one of a long and arduous journey's happy completion (earlier stages of the journey are depicted in the background). No less than the Magi, the very animals are overflowing with joy.

An important part of Gentile's *Adoration of the Magi* is the so-called predella, the section at the bottom with the three painted panels. This way of elucidating the main subject by means of glosses or "footnotes" goes back to Giotto's day. The idea was taken from manuscript illuminations and painted crucifixes to which miniature scenes from the Passion were attached at the sides of the body

Plate 21. Gentile da Fabriano. The Adoration of the Magi. 1423. Uffizi Gallery, Florence

and the ends of the cross piece. The three panels of Gentile's predella show the *Nativity,* "His light shining before them," at the left, *The Flight into Egypt* (the horizontal format bringing out the magnitude of the distance to be covered) in the center, and *The Presentation in the Temple* at right. (The original of the last-named is in the Louvre; the panel in the Uffizi Gallery is a copy.)

Giovanni di Paolo (1403–1483) was a Sienese artist of the old school, for all that Masaccio, Gozzoli, Castagno, and Piero della Francesca were his contemporaries. (These representatives of Renaissance painting will be discussed below.) He still paints in the narrative style of the late Gothic

period. The panel reproduced here (pl. 22) illustrates a passage from St. Mark's account of the death of Saint John the Baptist: "And the King sent his soldiers... and one of them went to the prison and cut off his head and brought the head on a platter." Various episodes of the martyrdom are depicted simultaneously and intended to be read as an epic sequence. But the viewer cannot help suspecting that the artist has lavished more affectionate concern on the architectural background than on the Biblical figures. The latter are all alike, and their expression of horror is stereotyped in theatrical gesture. In the architecture, however, the painter displays extraordinary in-

Plate 22. Giovanni di Paolo. The Head of Saint John the Baptist Brought before Herod. 1455–60.
Art Institute of Chicago. Mr. and Mrs. Martin A. Ryerson Collection

Plate 23. Masaccio. The Tribute Money (portion). c. 1428. Brancacci Chapel, Santa Maria del Carmine, Florence

ventiveness, creating a veritable *capriccio* of perspective views to suggest the vastness of Herod's palace.

THE EARLY RENAISSANCE IN FLORENCE

How different from the foregoing are Masaccio's frescoes in the Brancacci chapel (c. 1428)! Masaccio, born in Rome in 1401, made his home in Tuscany at an early age, and can be regarded as the virtual originator of early Renaissance painting in Florence. His frescoes in the Brancacci chapel of the church of Santa Maria del Carmine

in Florence can be taken as a declaration of his artistic principles. His figures have heavy, massive bodies, modeled in the round and firmly placed within a fully elaborated picture space. His compositions are powerful and well balanced, and his figures, related to one another by their gestures, are clearly grouped. In contrast to the Gothic narrative sequences by Giovanni di Paolo, Masaccio treats each episode as a self-contained pictorial unit. He also achieves a unified pictorial space by means of central perspective, lighting, the organization of the architectural elements, and an appropriate color scheme. Light and shadow obey the laws of nature. The expressiveness of color is increased. Subsidiary decorations are dispensed

31

Plate 24. Benozzo Gozzoli. The Procession of the Magi (portion). 1459–60. Medici Palace Chapel, Florence

with. It is instructive to compare Masaccio's work with Gherardo Starnina's frescoes in the same church, which were completed in 1404. Only fragments of isolated figures have survived, but these remains still show that the work was executed in the luminous "soft" style then in vogue. At the turn of the century Starnina was the main representative of the monumental traditional style, and Masaccio was probably impressed by his large, massive figures.

The detail of Masaccio's *The Tribute Money* (pl. 23) shows the "Receiver of the Double Drachmas" (the tax for maintenance of the temple) in front of Christ, with his back to the viewer. Christ is saying to St. Peter: "Notwithstanding, lest we should offend them, go thou to the sea, and cast an hook, and take up the fish that first cometh up; and when thou hast opened his mouth, thou shalt find a piece of money: that take, and give unto them for me and thee" (Matt. 17:27). This miracle is represented on the left side of the fresco (not shown in our detail). In this simultaneous representation of

different actions the painting is still old-fashioned. But there is tremendous power in the composition. The forms are built up by means of color only, without linear·contours or ornaments.

At the time Masaccio was clambering about the scaffolding in the Brancacci chapel, Benozzo Gozzoli was eight years old. One of the most popular fresco painters in his native Florence, he displayed an extraordinary talent for narrative pictures. His most important work is the decoration of the private chapel in the Palazzo Medici-Ricardi, in which he executed a colorful frieze representing the journey of the Magi (pl. 24). The painting was probably influenced by Gentile da Fabriano's altarpiece; it is also obvious that the artist was acquainted with Flemish tapestries.

The Medici Palace, built by the architect Michelozzo Michelozzi, was begun in 1444, and is the first truly Renaissance palace in Florence. Cosimo Medici the Elder commissioned Benozzo Gozzoli to decorate the palace chapel. Gozzoli (1420–1497) was then a young man working in Rome. His deco-

Plate 25. Andrea del Castagno. David. c. 1450–57. National Gallery of Art, Washington, D.C.

rations in the chapel were begun in 1459. At that time the room had no window, and he was forced to work for months by candlelight or with the aid of an oil lamp. The work was probably completed in 1460.

Followed by an impressive retinue and a crowd of commoners and nobles on foot and horseback, the Magi are shown on three sides of the room, coming down out of mountains, traveling through a Tuscan landscape. The episode is narrated in great detail, following the tradition of the Late Gothic style. The first of the kings, with a long white beard, is seen riding on a mule; the second has black hair and rides a white horse; the third is young and fair: this rider is a portrait of Lorenzo the Magnificent as a boy. On white horses with red bridles, in front of Lorenzo, come his three charming young sisters, Nannina, Bianca, and Maria. They are followed by their father Piero and grandfather Cosimo (who built the palace). This scene is especially reminiscent of Flemish tapestries, such as the one representing a falcon hunt, made at Tournai about 1440 (now in the Victoria and Albert Museum, London).

The frescoes in the chapel extend over an altar niche which contains a painting by Filippo Lippi. The original is now in Berlin, but a copy can be seen in the chapel. The subject is the Madonna and Child—goal of the long journey made by the three kings from the east.

Benozzo Gozzoli had a great many talented contemporaries, among others Paolo Uccello (1400–1475), Domenico Veneziano (1410–1461), Filippo Lippi (1406–1469), Antonio del Pollaiuolo (1429–1498), Andrea del Verrocchio (1435–1488), Sandro Botticelli (1444–1510), and Andrea del Castagno (1423–1457). The last mentioned worked in Florence. At the center of his compositions are always human figures, treated monumentally yet expressing their inner feelings. In his work shown here (pl. 25), David is represented as triumphant in victory, yet at the same time as a youth horrified by his own bloody exploit. The Biblical king was a popular subject, both for youthful grace and sensitive musicianship (see pl. 10) and for his great victory over Goliath. David was often included in the series of famous men that were popular in the fourteenth and fifteenth centuries, and was the most popular Old Testament hero. The unusual shape of this picture is due to the fact that it was painted on a leather shield which was designed to be carried in processions.

PIERO DELLA FRANCESCA

Piero della Francesca (1416–1492) was born at Borgo San Sepolcro and began to paint during Castagno's lifetime. As the leading artist of the Umbrian school during the Quattrocento (fifteenth century), one of the greatest painters Italy had so far produced, he succeeded in blending the manner of northern Italy, above all that of Venice, with the more sculptural Florentine manner. This synthesis is the heart of his highly personal style. A friend of Luca Pacioli, the famous mathematician and translator of Euclid, and author of a treatise titled *De divina proportione,* Piero was himself a learned theoretician of perspective, and he composed a three-volume textbook on this subject titled *De prospectiva pingendi.* It is hardly surprising, then, that his handling of space in his pictures should be so skillfully "natural" as to make us forget how "studied" they actually are. Piero della Francesca was also one of the first artists to tackle the typically modern problem of natural lighting in out-of-doors settings, a problem he addressed himself to deliberately and successfully.

The choir of the church of San Francesco in Arezzo contains the master's most impressive work—the monumental cycle of frescoes illustrating the legend of the Holy Cross. It was executed between 1454 and 1461. Ten panels relate the story of the Cross on which Christ died, from the time of Adam, when it was the tree of the knowledge of good and evil, down to the day when it was recovered from the heathen by the Emperor Constantine. For his narrative, Piero follows the *Golden Legend,* composed in Latin by Jacobus de Voragine in 1254 or shortly thereafter and translated into Italian as early as the fourteenth century. Pictorially, Piero's frescoes derive from two earlier Italian sequences illustrating the story of the Holy Cross: that by Agnolo Gaddi, which dates from the end of the fourteenth century, in the Franciscan church of Santa Croce in Florence, and that by Gaddi's pupil Cenni di Francesco di Ser Cenni, executed about 1420, in the chapel of the Compagnia di Santa Croce in the church of San Francesco in Volterra.

According to the legend, the tree which provided the wood for the Cross was to have served as a ceiling beam for Solomon's temple. After it was felled, however, it proved unusually hard, and so instead became a footbridge across a brook. When the Queen of Sheba came to Jerusalem to test the wisdom of Solomon by putting a series of riddles to him, she recognized in the trunk the fragment of wood from which the Cross was to be made. She knelt down and prophesied that one day a man put to death on a cross made from the wood of this very tree would cause the destruction of the kingdom of the Jews. Thereupon Solomon ordered the tree to be thrown into the Lake of Siloe. In two large horizontal panels situated under the story of Adam, the Queen of Sheba is shown kneeling, and meeting Solomon (pl. 26).

It is interesting to compare the panel reproduced here with Masaccio's *Tribute Money* (pl. 23) and Giotto's *Kiss of Judas* (pl. 19). Piero set the scene against a wall parallel to the picture plane. The stage on which the meeting is taking place is relatively shallow. The queen's ladies-in-waiting and

Plate 26. Piero della Francesca. Solomon and the Queen of Sheba. c. 1455. San Francesco, Arezzo

the king's councilors are grouped in semicircles behind their respective rulers. Whether facing us or turning their backs, these figures make a choreographic pattern that gives the illusion of a much vaster space—a device Giotto had already used for the figure on the left of his picture (pl. 19). Masaccio employed the device, too, but more dramatically: the tax collector is singled out by turning his back to the viewer, his face in profile. In Giotto's work the heads very nearly collide with each other in closely juxtaposed profile. This is, without doubt, a conscious artistic device for heightening tension. Piero presented the Queen of Sheba in profile for a similar reason: he wanted to bring out the difference between her enigmatic beauty and the heavy patriarchal figure of King Solomon.

By this time several schools of painting had arisen in other Italian towns, and some had already attained the peak of their development. Matteo di Giovanni still worked in Siena, although it had long since lost the pre-eminence it enjoyed in the fourteenth century. A contemporary of Matteo was the famous Francesco di Giorgio Martini (1439–

1502), architect, sculptor, and painter. The versatility he displayed was especially characteristic of the fifteenth century. Among the Umbrian painters who maintained workshops, next to Piero, we ought to mention Pietro Vannucci, called Perugino (1445–1523). We shall come across him here as the teacher of Raphael. Another artist of this school who deserves mention is Pinturicchio (1454–1530). With Perugino he decorated the Sistine chapel between 1480 and 1482, and he painted the famous frescoes in the Piccolomini Library of the cathedral of Siena between 1506 and 1508.

ANTONELLO DA MESSINA

Venetian painters of the period include Vivarini, Carlo Crivelli, Antonello da Messina (c. 1430–1479), the Bellini family, and Vittore Carpaccio (1455–1525).

The painting reproduced here, *Saint Sebastian,* is by Antonello, a much traveled master, whose works reflect the most varied influences (pl. 27).

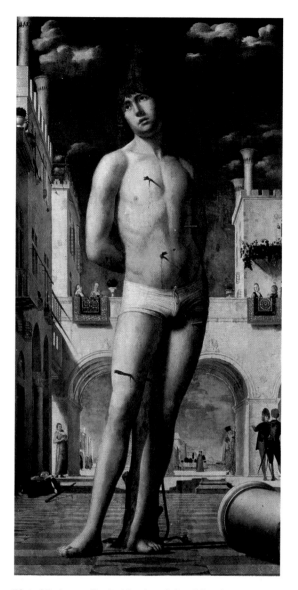

Plate 27. Antonello da Messina. Saint Sebastian.
c. 1475–79. Gemäldegalerie, Dresden

Pierced by many arrows, Saint Sebastian's ordeal was also his triumph: he died as a *martyros,* a witness to the truth. He has often been portrayed with a face like Christ's, to indicate that his suffering has been transcended in a higher order. The paintings illustrating the martyrdom of Saint Sebastian, like those depicting the Crucifixion, can be divided into two groups. In the first, the agony of martyrdom is stressed, suffering as the privilege of those who have been chosen for an uncommon fate. In the second the stress is on the beauty of man's triumph over suffering. This twofold approach raises both dogmatic and artistic problems.

Antonello da Messina painted this picture between 1475 and 1479. A Sicilian by birth (as his name

indicates), Antonello was living in Venice at the time. In the course of his travels he stayed some time in Naples. In Colantonio's workshop there and at King Alfonso's court he saw Flemish paintings, among them a picture by Jan van Eyck with many figures. According to Vasari, Antonello was a pupil of Van Eyck and introduced the Flemish oil technique into Italy. But the first part of this statement is obviously false: Antonello was born about 1430, and Jan van Eyck died in 1441. It is true, however, that when Antonello came to Venice in 1475, he had mastered the latest Flemish techniques of painting in oils. In his *Saint Sebastian* we discern, in addition to Flemish influences, those of his Italian contemporaries. Both Mantegna and

Plate 28. Andrea Mantegna. The Ascension. 1466–68. Uffizi Gallery, Florence

Piero della Francesca crossed his path before he died at Messina in 1479.

Antonello's work falls into the second of the two types of Saint Sebastians. Here he appears as a youth resigned to his fate: there is no sign of suffering; he has acquired inner mastery. With its abrupt perspective and extreme shifts of scale, this painting suggests the swift flight of arrows, five of which have hit their target. The mood of the painting is intensified by the boxed-in background space and the openings in it, through which clouds and unlimited skies are visible. The sight line in this picture is unusually low: we are at the height of the background figures and must raise our eyes to take in the martyred body and the head. The saint stands alone, barely noticed in a heartless world. The shaft of a broken column on the ground indicates that the martyrdom took place during pagan times, that it was the Empire that perished, not this witness to the new and ultimately triumphant faith.

ANDREA MANTEGNA

Antonello's contemporary Andrea Mantegna (1431–1506) was active in Padua, near Venice. His work profoundly influenced not just Italian artists, but also many painters in northern Europe, where it became known through engravings. No other painter of his time had a greater admiration for the art of the classical past than Mantegna. His teacher Francesco Squarcione—in this respect typical of university towns such as Padua—was interested in collecting antiquities and passed his interest on to his pupils. Mantegna himself owned a collection of ancient works.

In his paintings and frescoes, Mantegna achieved new heights of graphic plasticity through illusionism and figures modeled in the round. His architectural compositions, which evoke classical grandeur, his heroic background landscapes, his vivid colors (which extend Venetian influences into the second half of the century), and his sharp characterizations reflect the artist's passionate temperament and lofty idealism.

From 1457 on Mantegna worked in Mantua, at the court of the Gonzaga family. In 1467 he was in Florence, and from 1488 to 1489 he stayed in Rome, where he decorated the private chapel of Pope Innocent VIII in the Belvedere of the Vatican (the chapel has since been destroyed). The frescoes in the Ovetari chapel in the Eremitani church in Padua depict the legends of Saint Christopher and Saint James, and date from the period between 1449 and 1457. The representation of Saint James on his way to the place of execution is the first example of illusionism. The painting was intended to be viewed from the floor of the chapel, the viewer placed underneath it. The chapel was heavily damaged during World War II. The painting on the ceiling of the Camera degli Sposi (wedding

chamber) of the Ducal Palace in Mantua shows a balustraded pergola open to the blue sky above: girls and little angels look down on the viewer; a peacock sits on the balustrade—the illusion of an opening in the ceiling is admirably conveyed. Later, in the Baroque period, such illusionistic devices produce far more powerful effects—as of mighty orchestras, or of the heavens opening—but here in Mantegna's work we are treated to less shattering, chamber-music effects.

Mantegna's triptych in the Uffizi Gallery, of which the left wing showing the *Ascension* is reproduced here (pl. 28), was painted during his stay in Florence. The center panel depicts the *Adoration of the Magi,* and the one on the right the *Presentation in the Temple.* In 1495–96 Mantegna executed the *Madonna of Victory* (now in the Louvre), the first great painting representative of the cult of the Virgin, and the following year *Parnassus* (now in the Louvre), originally intended for the *studiolo* (study) of Isabella d'Este, the Marquise of Mantua.

RAPHAEL

To have examined several pictures of the Italian Renaissance will help us appreciate the work of the greatest artist of his time, Raphael of Urbino (1483–1520).

One of the first writers to recognize Raphael's greatness and to describe his works was Vasari. Like the painter's contemporaries, Vasari felt that Raphael's talent was a gift of God. "How generous and benevolent the heavenly powers can be at times," he wrote, "showering the wealth of their immense treasures and rare gifts (usually divided among many in the course of years) upon one man, was illustrated by the example of Raphael Sanzio of Urbino. Nature endowed him with love of his fellow men, and his gentle manner was combined with a gracious affability that made him treat all men with kindness and courtesy."

In his early years Raphael was trained by his father, with whom he executed his first works. Later he entered Perugino's workshop. Perugino, Raphael's real teacher, after years of traveling which took him to Florence and to Rome (where he helped decorate the Sistine chapel), settled in Perugia. Here the Montefeltro family generously supported the arts, attracting and encouraging north European as well as Italian painters. The Flemish heritage, so evident in the work of Perugino and Raphael, was transmitted to them by way of the court of Urbino. In frescoes and panels with spacious, brightly colored landscapes, Perugino expressed an ideal of serene beauty. The young Raphael imitated him, and his work soon became indistinguishable from that of his teacher. He broadened his somewhat provincial horizon when he went to Florence, the capital of Tuscan art. In 1508 he moved to Rome, where closer contact with

Plate 29. Raphael. The Marriage of the Virgin. 1504. Brera Gallery, Milan

Plate 30. Raphael. Madonna and Child (Colonna
Madonna). 1507–8. State Museums, Berlin-Dahlem

antiquity stimulated him to undertake new studies.
Commissioned soon after his arrival, by Pope
Julius II, to decorate his chambers in the Vatican,
Raphael painted the *School of Athens,* the *Disputa,*
and the *Expulsion of Heliodorus.* After the death
of the architect Donato Bramante in 1514, Raphael helped supervise the building of Saint Peter's.
He designed the cartoons for the tapestries in the
Sistine chapel, supervised decoration of the Vatican loggias, and worked at the *Galatea* cycle of
paintings in the Villa Farnese. In addition to these,
he painted many other works, among them the *Sistine Madonna,* a portrait of Julius II, and the *Madonna della Sedia,* the last-named in "tondo" or
round format—a format admired for its perfect
shape. In this painting, movement, form, and color
are brought into a particularly harmonious union.

Raphael's paintings were much in demand even in
his lifetime. Marcantonio Raimondi, one of the
inventors of copper engraving, was one of the first
to make engravings of Raphael's works, and so
they became available to a wider public.

Vasari, who popularized the mistaken idea that
art is the imitation of nature, also popularized
another prejudice, namely, that there is such a
thing as "progress" in art. According to him, art
developed from the most primitive beginnings
(Cimabue) to its highest flowering (Raphael, Michelangelo). This opinion furthered the belief that

art had attained perfection only in Italy in the first
half of the sixteenth century. It is true, of course,
that striving for formal perfection was particularly evident in Italy at that time. Indeed, the
friendly rivalry with antiquity—the attempts to
surpass Greek and Roman models—makes a fascinating subject for art historians. What is most
striking, however—especially in connection with
Raphael—is that artists come closest to the classical ideal when they most freely follow their own
inspiration.

How early Raphael was striving to attain perfect
form is strikingly illustrated by a youthful work,
now in the Brera Gallery: the altarpiece with the
Marriage of the Virgin (pl. 29). He painted it originally for the Church of San Francesco in Città di
Castello. The polygonal temple in the background
bears the proud inscription: "Raphael Urbinas
MDIIII."

This work of 1504 brings to mind the pieces that
were executed by journeymen artists in order to
obtain the title of "master." It proves convincingly
not only that Raphael was already a virtuoso de-
signer of circular buildings (greatly admired at
the time because a round plan was considered the
ideal architectural form), but also a painter of con-
summate skill at combining individual figures in a
memorably rhythmic group.

This painting, which incidentally imitates a similar

composition by Perugino, discloses an idealizing tendency. The prismatic perfection of the sixteen-sided temple on its pedestal of steps, and the precise extension of the red squares back into the distance, is even further emphasized by the strong symmetry of the whole design. The foreground figures, again symmetrically organized, are beautiful, unblemished people whose grace and ease is beyond the human range.

One of the "mortal gods," as Vasari called him, Raphael was most famous for his Madonnas. His feeling for form and his talent as a lyrical artist of inexhaustible imagination are particularly evident in his treatments of this subject. He varies the motif of the Virgin and Child from work to work, even omitting the traditional attributes on occasion, as in the *Colonna Madonna* (pl. 30). The painting (now in Berlin) is unfinished; a few layers of blue are missing. All the same, the *Colonna Madonna* and the *Madonna del Baldacchino* (Pitti Palace, Florence) are the greatest achievements of Raphael's Florentine period (1500–1508).

In some of his paintings of the Madonna and Child, Raphael presents them with saints to right and left, or alone with a youthful Saint John. Saint Joseph is occasionally included. We recognize the saints by their delicate halos. The work shown here, however, is one of those in which Raphael renounces all the more traditional touches. When we compare it with the *Madonna and Child* (pl. 16) painted shortly before the appearance of Giotto, we realize to what an extent the image of the Madonna had been transformed in the course of two centuries. The older picture shows her on a throne, which symbolizes the majesty of the Mother of God; in Raphael's picture she is shown against a background of nature, as a pretty young mother distracted from her reading by the child she holds lovingly on her lap. In the earlier picture the child is just a small adult, whereas Raphael gives us a lively little boy innocent of any vocation as Redeemer.

According to the German Romantic painter Alfred Rethel, the child in Raphael's *Sistine Madonna* (painted 1513–15 for San Sisto in Piacenza and now in Dresden) conveys a deeper meaning than the child in this earlier Florentine work. "The child's expression," he wrote, "is almost unbearable. The whole world is in his eyes. This child is already the Redeemer who will sacrifice himself to atone for the sins of mankind, already sitting at the Last Judgment. As one looks, the eyes blaze up, become bigger and bigger, and the lips seem to move. But most shattering of all is the outward calm of this extraordinary child. Though the arms and legs are still, they are alive thanks to the exquisite modeling." Of the Virgin in this painting Rethel says: "She is the Queen of Heaven, much more than a loving mother.... What a master! No doubt he was vouchsafed a vision, for he painted this in a single creative surge, dispensing with preliminary studies and oblivious to the world around him."

VERROCCHIO AND LEONARDO

Andrea del Verrocchio (1438–1488) was the kind of universal genius which only the Renaissance produced. His talents include sculpture, painting, the goldsmith's art, wood carving, music, and mathematics. He was the greatest sculptor among his Florentine contemporaries and no less famous as a painter. Leonardo da Vinci learned painting in his workshop—a fact of the greatest interest where Leonardo's early work is concerned. *The Baptism of Christ* (pl. 31) is generally regarded as Verrocchio's most important painting, although the attribution to him is not based on written evidence. We do not know precisely when it was painted, who commissioned it, where it was to go, or what decorative function it was to serve. In both editions of his *Lives,* Vasari says that Leonardo had a hand in *The Baptism of Christ*, namely, that he painted one of the angels. In his life of Leonardo, Vasari says that when confronted with the genius of his pupil, Verrocchio gave up painting.

The baptism takes place in a river flowing through a rocky landscape. At the center, the figure of Christ is presented full length, nearly in full face, his hands clasped in prayer. Above him we see the dove representing the Holy Spirit and the hands of God the Father in the gesture of blessing. Saint John is moving closer to the Saviour, and, like Him, is standing ankle-deep in water. The baptismal rite is being performed. At left, two angels without wings are kneeling on the riverbank. The strangeness of the landscape in which these figures are placed intensifies the mood of the picture.

Stylistic comparison between the angel shown in profile in this painting, and authenticated works by Leonardo, confirm Vasari's attribution of the figure to Leonardo, here in the process of becoming the greatest master of his day. This attribution is further supported by documentary evidence that Leonardo was active in Verrocchio's workshop as early as 1470. In 1472 he enrolled in the brotherhood of Saint Luke, but in 1476 he is mentioned as living in his teacher's house.

The earliest Florentine altarpiece on this subject, *The Baptism of Christ,* must have been executed at this time and worked over by Leonardo, who besides painting the one angel must also have had a hand in the strange landscape, for it strongly brings to mind landscapes in later works known to be by him, such as the *Mona Lisa* (pl. 32), *The Madonna and Child with Saint Anne,* and *The Virgin of the Rocks.*

Leonardo was born in 1452 at Vinci near Empoli. He was the single most versatile figure in the entire Renaissance. Not only did he master all the knowledge of his age, he also enlarged it considerably by his own researches and experiments. Besides practicing several arts (he was an architect and sculptor as well as a painter), he composed a treatise on painting, and one on aesthetics in which he discusses his own works. In addition to this he left

Plate 31. Andrea del Verrocchio. The Baptism of Christ. c. 1476. Uffizi Gallery, Florence

up a ladder, and Michelangelo would hold out a hand to help him up the scaffolding. But the Pope felt the work was taking too long. He ordered Michelangelo to unveil the painting when only the first part was completed. The people of Rome greatly admired the artist, and they flocked to the chapel no less eagerly than the Pope, almost before the dust raised by the removal of the scaffolding had settled."

No other work in the Western world has been so much reproduced, written about, and commented upon as the ceiling of the Sistine Chapel. Even the art specialists of our day have not exhausted it.

One of the most monumental figures on the ceiling is that of Jeremiah sunk in sorrowful thought (pl. 34). Michelangelo presents him in the spirit of the prophet's Lamentations, through which he entered the consciousness of mankind. With Michelangelo we have reached the threshold of a new age.

HIEREMIAS

Plate 34. Michelangelo. Jeremiah, from the ceiling of the Sistine Chapel. 1508–12. The Vatican, Rome

The Beginnings of Flemish and French Painting

The art of the Middle Ages and the Renaissance cannot be properly understood without reference to regional traditions. We recognize works related to one another when their forms are derived from common models. Each formal element exists in numerous variants which exhibit similar stylistic and compositional features. Fidelity to the tradition of a given "school" is reflected in a specific store of motifs that recur continually, the forms changing over a period of time. The system of the "schools" rests primarily on imitation (Perugino, Raphael). European painting falls into "schools" in this sense well into the Renaissance. In Italy, however, although even there a strict adherence to rules survived, certain artists came to display individual freedom earlier than elsewhere, which resulted in mannerism.

Not only apprentices but also master artists imitated such forms and formulas as were available, when this seemed appropriate. From the point of view of art criticism, what matters is a given artist's conception of "imitation." For example, the countless copies of drawings and engravings by Schongauer and Dürer are of little interest. However, Nicola Pisano's treatment of details he copied from ancient sarcophagi, Herlin's copies of motifs from Rogier van der Weyden, and Dürer's imitations and interpretations of Mantegna are something else again. Here the artists display real independence: instead of mechanically reproducing their models, they adapt them to their own individual modes of expression. It is important to keep all this in mind when we study the following examples of old Flemish painting dating from the close of the Middle Ages.

The beginnings of northern European painting in the fifteenth century are best illustrated by works that originated in the Low Countries and northern France. From 1400 on, we witness a stirring spectacle: the gradual conquest of light and space, first in manuscript illumination, and then in easel painting.

Let us begin with *The Flight into Egypt* (pl. 35) by Melchior Broederlam, a native of Ypres, where he was active between 1381 and 1409. It is one of the four scenes from the life of Mary which constituted an altarpiece. The artist represents the scene as viewed from above. The Holy Family in flight is depicted with attention to minute detail. Mary with the Child in her arms is quietly sitting on the donkey while Joseph quenches his thirst. The figures are carefully characterized, and the landscape is shown in the sharpest possible definition. We clearly make out rocks and trees, but background and foreground lie in the same plane. The landscape unfolds in height, not in depth.

If we compare this work with Simone Martini's *Christ Bearing the Cross* (pl. 20), painted about eighty years earlier, the most obvious differences can only be interpreted as advances in the feeling for nature. In Simone Martini's scene we also view the scene somewhat from above, and every face in the crowd passing through the gate is clearly visible. The buildings in the background appear in a complicated but disjointed perspective, and the gold ground precludes any sense of depth.

Now let us anticipate for a moment, and compare the fourteenth-century work with one painted about a hundred years later. In *Rest on the Flight into Egypt* by Joachim Patinir (pl. 45), whom Dürer considered an outstanding landscape painter, the figures are shown in a landscape which unfolds gradually from a detailed foreground to blue mountains and a sky with clouds in the distance. Now seen as a continuum, space can be rendered in depth with the aid of techniques developed between 1400 and 1500.

The *Très Riches Heures du Duc de Berry,* dating from 1413–16, is an important landmark in this development. *Winter* (pl. 36), the illustration for the month of February in this ducal Book of Hours, shows (once more from above) a farm with a hilly wintry landscape beyond it. The pictorial space is still somewhat discontinuous: the family in front of the fireplace, the birds in the snow, the sheep huddled together in their fold, the man felling a tree, the donkey driver—all these details are merely juxtaposed, not subordinated to an over-all pictorial conception. Each is meant to be read as a separate "sentence," as it were, their sum total making a picture representing Winter. The figure of the man with the donkey is especially instructive. Surprisingly big, he so to speak links the middle ground to the foreground, and so prevents the eye from being too promptly directed to the village in the distance.

Plate 35. Melchior Broederlam. The Flight into Egypt (portion). c. 1394. Musée des Beaux-Arts, Dijon

Plate 36. Limbourg Brothers. Winter (February), from Les Très Riches Heures du Duc de Berry. 1413–16. Musée Condé, Chantilly

THE PATRONS

The Duc de Berry was one of the most prominent patrons of the arts in the early fifteenth century. By the time he died (in 1415) the arts were more actively encouraged in Burgundy than in France proper. The Charterhouse outside of Dijon was an important artistic center under the first dukes of Burgundy (who were Valois). The monastery was founded by Philip the Bold in 1383, its church designed as a memorial to his rule, and he was buried there.

The artistic activity involved in building and decorating the Charterhouse brought fame to Dijon. A number of Swiss and South German painters are known to have traveled *gon Dision* (to Dijon) to get an idea of the latest developments in the art of painting. When Hans von Tiefenthal was commissioned to decorate a chapel in Basel, he was told to paint like the artists "at Dijon in the Charterhouse monastery."

In the next few decades, wherever Burgundian rule prevailed, painting achieved a brilliance comparable only to the contemporaneous achievements of Florentine masters. Although the house of Burgundy did not initiate the developments in painting associated with its name, it did a great deal to further them.

The social structure of the region stretching from the Low Countries to Burgundy was rich in tensions. Not only the dukes, but also their ministers and courtiers became patrons of the arts. During the reign of Philip the Good (pl. 37), the situation was roughly as follows: At the head of the patrons was the duke himself, powerful and wealthy enough to employ artists on his private account. Next in rank to him was his chancellor, Nicolas Rolin, who founded the hospital at Beaune and commissioned Rogier van der Weyden to paint an altarpiece representing the *Last Judgment*. After Rolin came Chevrot, Bishop of Tournai and chairman of the Grand Council, and Pieter Bladelin, the duke's treasurer, who also commissioned Rogier van der Weyden to paint an altarpiece (now in Berlin). A miniature in the *Chroniques du Hainault* shows the Duke of Burgundy and the above-mentioned dignitaries (pl. 38).

The ranks of the patrons were swelled by rich merchants, mostly Italians who opened branches of their businesses in the north. One of them was Arnolfini, immortalized in Jan van Eyck's *Giovanni Arnolfini and His Bride*. Another was Portinari, who commissioned Van der Goes to paint an altarpiece for a church in Florence. A third was Tani, a cloth merchant who sold silk from Lucca and brocade from Genoa in the Low Countries.

Soon the cities themselves began to rival the rich merchants in giving commissions to artists. Brussels persuaded Rogier van der Weyden to work for it, and Louvain enjoyed the services of Dirc Bouts. Burghers who were less well-to-do were nonetheless able to commission large works through the guilds and societies they belonged to.

The most famous painter at the Burgundian court was Jan van Eyck. Since he was in the employ of such eminent patrons as the Duke himself, he could disregard the medieval restrictions imposed on other artists by the guilds, and so break with tradition. It was not by chance that Vasari referred to him as the inventor of oil painting, the new *pictura lucida* with its glowing colors and carefully differentiated textures. On May 19, 1425, Jan van Eyck entered the service of Philip the Good. His title was *peintre et valet de chambre*, and his salary a hundred *livres* a year. His status must have been exceptional, since the duke entrusted him on several occasions with secret political missions. Two centuries later, at the beginning of his artistic career, Peter Paul Rubens held a similar diplomatic post.

Experience gained through travel is reflected in the *Ghent Altarpiece,* painted by the brothers Hubert and Jan van Eyck in 1431. This monumental painting was the last important work to be created in the spirit of medieval devotion.

The painting done for the Burgundian court displays specific features not often found in painting done for other north European courts. The courtly tradition expressed itself not only in emphasis upon finery and elegant bearing, but also in the iconography or, more accurately, in the way old motifs were transformed and adapted to secular needs. Religious motifs were adapted to the representation of court life in a picture of the *Adoration of the Magi,* for example, in which we see the Duke himself accompanied by his greyhound. Similarly, the motif of *virgo inter virgines*—the Virgin among virgins—is transformed to present Mary as queen, the martyred virgins around her represented as ladies-in-waiting displaying the dainty manner then prescribed by the court etiquette.

One branch of painting practiced at the court with particular skill was portraiture, which was also a favorite with the rising middle class. Pious Christians had themselves portrayed with breviaries in hand, scholars with their rolls of parchment, pens, and ink wells. Women were portrayed as virtuous wives and mothers at the spinning wheel or with their sewing baskets. Noblemen always carry a sword and often wear a helmet. Men shown reading letters or presenting a petition were persons of special influence. Commoners, too, had their portraits painted: the architect with his measuring rod, the surgeon with his forceps, the mathematician with his compass, the scientist with his glass or metal retort. Needless to say, these pictorial attributes were simply secularized versions of those long employed to represent saints and other figures of the Christian pantheon.

All the same, the greatest achievement of Burgundian courtly art was manuscript illumination. The production of book illustrations and ornamental lettering was enormous: Bibles, psalters, Books of Hours, prayerbooks, books on classical mythology,

Plate 37. Copy after Rogier van der Weyden. Philip the Good. Original c. 1445. Groeningemuseum, Bruges

Plate 38. Dedication Page from the Chroniques du Hainault. 1446. Bibliothèque Royale, Brussels

the lives of heroes, even contemporary chronicles. Few even today recognize the scale of production at this time. In 1463 David Aubert described the library at the court of Burgundy, founded a hundred years earlier, as "the richest and most noble library in the world." A few years later the library contained 900 volumes, most of them illustrated with miniatures. Among the secular books, the chronicles and *romans d'aventure* (tales of adventure) are specially remarkable.

It is interesting to compare *February* from the *Très Riches Heures du Duc de Berry* (pl. 36) with Van Eyck's *The Three Marys at the Tomb* (pl. 39). In the center of Van Eyck's panel is the empty tomb. The white angel seated upon the displaced lid of the tomb is telling the three Marys that Christ has risen from the dead. The three sleeping soldiers lie between the viewer and the heavenly messenger. The background is clearly set off from the rest of the picture by rocks, which serve as a frame for the action in the center. Far in the distance the city of Jerusalem is visible, represented as a medieval town on a hillside with highly

imaginative architecture. Snow-capped mountains merging with the sky mark the extreme boundary of the landscape.

THE CONQUEST OF SPACE

The correct co-ordination between figures and space was first mastered in paintings of interiors. An example is Rogier van der Weyden's *The Annunciation* (pl. 40). Certain works by earlier painters, such as the Master of Flémalle, could have served equally well. The figures of Mary and the Angel are correctly scaled to the proportions of the bedroom here depicted in loving detail. The same system of perspective prevails everywhere in the picture. The doorway with the bench against it has been handled with almost pedantic correctness. The reason painters at this time suddenly managed to render figures in space instead of against an artificial setting may be that they worked almost exclusively in their studios, and

Plate 39. Hubert and/or Jan van Eyck. The Three Marys at the Tomb. c. 1430. Boymans-van Beuningen Museum, Rotterdam

that they portrayed familiar objects of everyday life. In landscapes, however, they still relied largely on memory and imagination, and followed pictorial conventions just as medieval artists had done.

Rogier van der Weyden's *The Entombment* (pl. 41) shows the influence of the Florentine Fra Angelico, and there are other reminiscences of Italy as well in this picture. In the Papal Jubilee year of 1450, Rogier was in Rome. His painting is the earliest, among those reproduced in this book, in which the landscape is continuous in space, unfolding naturally into depth. At the left of the hill in which the tomb is set we see a road with figures walking on it, which leads from Golgotha toward Jerusalem, whose mighty buildings are visible in the background. In this work Rogier exploits a device painters had already been using at the beginning of the century: the road is intended to serve as an optical guide line, the figures traversing it in the middle distance bigger than those behind them, in this case a man on horseback. Thanks to such perspective devices the artists became capable of

representing a segment of the visible world in one unified composition.

Besides this essentially linear device, others were invented at this time, which helped transform the picture area into a space of almost limitless depth. Dirc Bouts' *Moses before the Burning Bush* (pl. 42) makes an excellent case in point. In addition to lines that lead the eye from left and right into the background, Bouts also makes use of color to convey the sense of depth: he does not just vary lights and darks; the browns and greens of the foreground shade gradually into pure greens and finally into blues. The latter color softened with white produces the impression that the mountains in the background are slowly dissolving in shimmering sunshine.

Although this investment of landscape with atmospheric depth marks an advance, the handling of the figures seems curiously old-fashioned. Two episodes of the story are represented simultaneously: the seated Moses taking off his shoes in the middle ground is the same Moses who stands barefoot in the foreground, startled by his vision,

Plate 40. Rogier van der Weyden. The Annunciation (portion). c. 1434–35. The Louvre, Paris

Plate 41. Rogier van der Weyden. The Entombment. c. 1450. Uffizi Gallery, Florence

Plate 42. Dirc Bouts. Moses before the Burning Bush. c. 1470. Philadelphia Museum of Art. John G. Johnson Collection

and about to fall on his knees before the Burning Bush. This manner of simultaneously staging, so to speak, several acts of a drama in a single picture had long been practiced. It must be interpreted as an attempt to introduce the dimension of time into painting. Had Moses' vision alone been shown, only a limited span of time would have been represented, but because we also see an earlier scene, the limit of time is pushed further into the past. The purpose here is not to heighten the drama of a single event, but to broaden the epic narrative.

JEAN FOUQUET

The innovations of the Flemish painters, which amount to a conquest of pictorial space, marked a revolutionary break with the medieval conception of painting. Something similar was going on in France. One of the earliest and finest landscape painters was Jean Fouquet (c. 1420–1480).

Despite Fouquet's considerable output, hardly anything is known about his early life and training. It is generally assumed that before going to Italy he had been an apprentice painter in Paris, where he acquainted himself with the great French tradition of manuscript illumination. In the course of the Hundred Years' War, the kings of France were obliged to move from Paris to the banks of the Loire: from Charles VII to Francis I, France was ruled from Blois and Amboise. This was how Tours, second only to Paris in size, became an important artistic center in the second half of the fifteenth century. When Fouquet came back from Rome, he did not go to Paris but settled in his native Touraine. His cycle of miniatures, including the Old Testament series *Antiquités Judaïques* (pl. 43), executed between 1460 and 1470, makes the final (and the greatest) chapter in the history of French illumination. At the time Fouquet began to work in Tours, Johann Gutenberg was developing the technique of printing from movable type in Mainz. This invention, together with the development of engraving on wood and copper, was eventually to supplant hand-painted illustration, the so-called "illuminated" book. Thus Fouquet stands at a turning point in history: he was the last great *peintre et enlumineur*. It is interesting to note that French illumination came to an end in the same Tours where it began in the Carolingian period. The first such works were produced under the Abbot Vivian around 800, in the age of Alcuin. The earliest Bibles decorated with figures date from about 850. The first painter of the "school of Tours" was a monk; his most important work is the Bible of Charles the Bald with its famous dedicatory leaf and methodical layout. The art of illumination in the West went back to fifth-century Byzantine models, and so was linked up with the classical tradition. As the last great illuminator 600 years later, Jean Fouquet was thus an heir to the painters of Greece and Rome, though he came by his inheritance in a roundabout fashion.

Jean Fouquet was the greatest single exponent of this originally French (indeed, Touraine) "art of the miniature." He carried as far as it could go the representation in line and color of minutely depicted actions in the tiny format suitable to manuscript pages. His greatness lies in the way he triumphs over technical limitations. Despite the tiny format, he frequently achieves monumentality. Using a brush consisting of one or two hairs, he brings natural vitality even to the most incidental of his book illustrations, and dispenses entirely with flashy, purely ornamental effects, such as those achieved by the use of gold backgrounds.

The traditional gold grounds were going out of fashion in Fouquet's day in painting proper as well as in book illustration. Konrad Witz, a contemporary of Fouquet, painted the first truly identifiable landscape in 1444, as one part of his altarpiece in Geneva. He set the New Testament episode of the *Miraculous Draught of Fishes* against the lakefront in Geneva, with Hermance, Mont Blanc, and Mont Salève in the background. Fouquet makes a similar use of actual landscapes a few years later. His views of Paris, which he knew well, are famous. In works of this kind, which can be related to the practice of earlier book illustration, Fouquet often chooses an elevated viewpoint. In his *The Conquest of Jericho* (pl. 43) we see not only the whole of the besieging army but also the entire town, plus a surrounding landscape which has the topographical features of the Loire valley.

The remarkable depth in Fouquet's picture reflects his profound knowledge of perspective. His mastery of it enables him to achieve a natural presentation of the relations between human figures and their natural or man-made settings. Like the Flemish painters, Fouquet favors aerial perspective. His colors are saturated in the foreground, less dense in the middle distance, and in the back of his landscape they dissolve into dazzling blue skies.

Fouquet's miniatures take any amount of enlargement without losing any of their power or persuasiveness. Where they really begin to rival easel paintings, however, they reveal their natural limitations. What characterizes medieval manuscript painting is that action is represented parallel to the picture surface, on a flat monochrome or golden ground. As soon as perspective makes its appearance on the manuscript page, the miniature loses its originally decorative and ornamental function. But Fouquet was not only a miniaturist, he also created excellent easel paintings. As *peintre* he stood at the beginning of a glorious development, as *enlumineur* he was the last and greatest exponent of a dying art.

Plate 43. Jean Fouquet. The Conquest of Jericho. Illustration from Les Antiquités Judaïques. c. 1475. Bibliothèque Nationale, Paris

Plate 44. Hieronymus Bosch. The Hay Wain. c. 1490.
The Prado, Madrid

THE GREAT NARRATIVE PAINTERS

To conclude our survey of old Flemish painting, we shall discuss works by three masters. All of them were highly imaginative narrators and display in varying degrees a predilection for the fantastic and the comical.

Hieronymus Bosch (c. 1450–1516), "the founding father of oneiric and grotesque painting," transports us to surrealistic realms. The figures of a sick fancy in *The Temptation of Saint Anthony,* and his visions of heaven and hell in other works unfold before the spellbound viewer as magnificent spectacles crammed with sinister, disquieting details.

Little of Bosch's life is known. Although his work draws upon all the resources of medieval allegory, and from one point of view his art is the culmination of this older tradition, he actually created something entirely new. Endowed with an extraordinary imagination, he explored what lies hidden behind the surface of things; his vision illustrates one of the basic tendencies in European painting, one that recurs again and again, and since Bosch has erupted in Goya, Alfred Kubin, Max Ernst, among many others. *The Hay Wain* (pl. 44) is the center panel of a triptych which translates into the language of painting the Flemish proverb: "The whole world is a haycart, let everyone get as much of it as he can." Demons and condemned sinners,

half human and half beast, are pulling the heavy cart along the road to hell. A frenzied crowd with ladders and pitchforks is making a rush for the hay, which symbolizes all the good things of this transient world.

Joachim Patinir (c. 1480–1524) received the title Master of Painting in Antwerp in 1515. Together with his German contemporary Albrecht Altdorfer, he greatly advanced landscape painting, though landscape had appeared in miniature painting shortly after 1500. A work like his *Rest on the Flight into Egypt* (pl. 45) gives us a vast panorama extending far into depth, viewed from above with a high horizon line. The human figures are purely accessories. Characteristic of Patinir's style are the rocks and mountains rising steeply out of a charming river valley. Like the Tower of Babel painted by Pieter Bruegel (c. 1520–1569), they reach into the clouds.

The Tower of Babel (pl. 46) dates from 1563, but the earliest written mention is by the Dutch biographer Carel van Mander. In his *Schilderboek* he wrote: "Some of his [Bruegel's] most important works are now owned by the Emperor [Rudolf II]. One of them, a *Tower of Babel,* is full of beautiful detail."

On a rocky headland by the sea, the tower, supported by mighty foundations, rises steeply into the sky. The very top is above the clouds. As the

Plate 45. Joachim Patinir. Rest on the Flight into Egypt. c. 1510. State Museums, Berlin-Dahlem

eye winds around the continuous ramp that spirals upward, successive round arches, blind arcades, moldings, little balconies, and buttresses present us with an anthology of Romanesque architecture. Part of the tower is cut away so we can glimpse concentric arcades recalling Roman amphitheaters. It is conjectured that here Bruegel was influenced by the Colosseum, which he saw when he visited Rome; but he was probably also influenced by Oriental models.

The giant Nimrod, the king of Babylon who built the tower, can be seen in the lower left foreground. Masons are prostrating themselves before him.

Behind the tower is a walled town. In the right foreground we see the harbor with sailing ships lying at anchor, and a busy quarry where stone blocks are being cut and shaped. The cranes which lift the masonry to vertiginous heights are worked by treadmills.

We shall come back to Pieter Bruegel in discussing a development leading to Rembrandt and the great narrative painters of the seventeenth century. In Bruegel's art we can still detect traces of the Middle Ages, but in him we also sense the opening of a new era, reaching to the very threshold of our own day.

Plate 46. Pieter Bruegel the Elder. The Tower of Babel (portion). 1563. Kunsthistorisches Museum, Vienna

Plate 47. Master Bertram. Cain Slaying Abel, from the Saint Peter's Altar. 1379. Kunsthalle, Hamburg

Plate 48. Stefan Lochner. The Virgin of the Rose Garden. c. 1440. Wallraf-Richartz Museum, Cologne

German Painting between 1400 and 1600

As early as the fourteenth century, easel painting began to assume growing importance in Germany. The influence of French book illumination and Italian painting contributed both to more vigorous, more meaningful pictorial forms and to the development of the "soft" or international Gothic style that was current in other countries around 1400.

THE "SOFT" STYLE

Bohemia was one of the centers of the International Style in northeastern Europe. Charles IV made Prague an artistic capital. While Charles was chiefly interested in architecture, his successor Wenzel encouraged the minor arts, including manuscript painting: the illuminated books made

for him are among the finest examples of the International Style, which has been exemplified here by the works of Melchior Broederlam (pl. 35) and Gentile da Fabriano (pl. 21). In other artistic centers, too, works were created which incorporate elements of local traditions, and which are among the noblest products of German art. The anonymous Master of Saint Veronica was active in Cologne; Master Bertram and Konrad von Soest were active in Westphalia; Master Francke in Hamburg, and the Master of the *Paradiesgärtlein* (*Little Garden of Paradise*) in the Upper Rhine region. The new manner combined Gothic linear rhythms with a newly developed sense of the forms and colors of the visible world. Among the distinguishing marks of this early fifteenth-century art is an obvious pleasure in delicate, childlike effects. Even in so dramatic a work as *Cain Slaying Abel*

Plate 49. Konrad Witz. Saint Christopher. c. 1435.
Öffentliche Kunstsammlung, Basel

(pl. 47) by Master Bertram (c. 1367–1450), the cruelty of the subject is completely overshadowed by the "softness" of the style. The melodious flowing curves of the figures are hardly in keeping with the dramatic action. Characteristic of Bertram's style, which also shows traces of Bohemian influences, are the compact, plastic forms and the striking colors. His principal surviving works are the *Grabow Altarpiece* from which the painting shown here is taken, *The Passion* from the altar of the Johanneskirche in Hamburg (now in the Landesmuseum, Hanover), and the *Buxtehude Altar* of about 1400 (now in the Kunsthalle, Hamburg).

Stefan Lochner was the greatest painter of the School of Cologne. His works mark a late and precious flowering of the International Style. *The Virgin of the Rose Garden* (pl. 48), executed around 1440, shows the Madonna and Child surrounded by very young angels playing musical instruments. The picture is of the type used for devotional purposes, which invites the viewer to meditate on the mystery of the Immaculate Conception.

KONRAD WITZ

Parallel with the soft style, an opposite "harder" tendency asserted itself in the first half of the fif-

teenth century. It marks the attempt to portray a new reality. This is the naturalistic strand of Late Gothic art which seeks to arrive at a truer portrayal of earthly existence with its use of angular interlocking forms. In Germany, new formulations of this interpretation of reality are found above all in the *Magdalen Altarpiece* (1431) by Lucas Moser at Tiefenbronn, and the so-called *Geneva Altar* (1444) by Konrad Witz. The influence of Flemish painters can be traced as early as the generation of Konrad Witz, whose *Saint Christopher* is reproduced here (pl. 49), and from the middle of the century on it is dominant. Works by Rogier van der Weyden and Dirc Bouts, especially, found enthusiastic imitators. The Flemish style directly or indirectly (through traveling artists) influenced a number of German schools, giving rise to pictorial inventions adapted to the conditions and tastes of other parts of Europe. The most notable exponents were Hans Pleydenwurff and Michael Wohlgemut in Franconia, Jan Polak in Bavaria, Hans Schüchlin, Friedrich Herlin, and Bartolomäus Zeitblom in Swabia, Martin Schongauer in the Upper Rhine valley, the Master of the Darmstadt Passion in the Middle Rhine valley, and the Master of the Life of Mary in Cologne.

The last-named master's *Annunciation* (pl. 50), dating from about 1460, conveys an idea of his potentialities and limitations. In pictorial quality his

Plate 50. The Master of the Life of Mary. The Annunciation. c. 1460. Alte Pinakothek, Munich

works are in no way inferior to those of the Flemish artists. The setting of the *Annunciation* was without doubt inspired by the theater of the period. The interior is cursorily sketched with a few props: a bench with cushions, a *prie-dieu*. The Annunciation takes place in this confined space. Disturbed at her devotions by the voice of the angel, Mary turns toward the messenger in a humble attitude, while her left hand marks the place in the book where her reading was interrupted. The angel has entered from the left and is moving with gentle determination toward her.

Works of this kind seem no more than preludes to Dürer's magnificent accomplishments. He was a universal genius capable of incarnating the spirit of an entire age.

ALBRECHT DÜRER

Everything that agitated or concerned men around 1500 was reflected in Dürer's paintings and prints: evocations of classical antiquity, the Bible story and legends of the saints, contemporary political events and personalities. His art expresses a new world and his encyclopedic output includes elements of sheer invention, lived experience, and borrowings from older works which he remade thoroughly, enhancing their artistic qualities and clarifying their meanings.

Albrecht Dürer (1473–1528) was born in Nuremberg, into a century which had begun with the Council of Constance (1414–18), saw the fall of Constantinople (1453), and closed with a new conception of the world ushered in by Copernicus and the discovery of America. Within Dürer's lifetime fall the first voyage around the world (1519–22) the Peasant War in Germany (1524–25), and the sack of Rome by the troops of Charles V (1527). Dürer was aware of the occupation of Hungary by the Turks, and was drawn into the vortex of the Reformation toward the end of his life.

This period of burning issues, passions, and conflicts between armed ideological camps, and a Church weakened by internal abuses, was at the same time the age when Germany became conscious of its separate identity even as it became acquainted with Italian Humanism and the Renaissance. The effect was to secularize men's conception of their place in the world; long-established beliefs now began to be discarded or reformulated in the light of new ideas.

How exciting it must have been to live in the first flush of this new worldview! It is true that Jan van Eyck had earlier painted a miniature atlas for Philip the Good, Duke of Burgundy—but now Martin Behaim of Nuremberg constructed the first globe, and

Plate 51. Albrecht Dürer. Self-Portrait. 1498. The Prado, Madrid

everybody knew that the earth was round and merely a small part of a *mysterium cosmographicum* (as Kepler put it in 1596). Life on earth now seemed subordinated to new universal laws.

All this must be kept in mind in order to understand Dürer's works of the "Heaven and Earth" type, in which the picture is divided into a heavenly and earthly domain, each perfectly distinct from the other yet to be seen as a whole, a cosmos, the totality of all things. Yet there are signs of an impending end of the world in Dürer's heaven. His skies are often darkened by sinister clouds in which mysterious images take shape presaging the Biblical Apocalypse.

Italy had her Dante, and her artists illustrated the *Inferno* of his *Divine Comedy*. Germany had the *Apocalypse,* a sequence of woodcuts on this subject which Dürer published at his own expense, and which became so popular that he prepared a second edition in 1511. As early as 1515 the prints were being issued "under license" in Venice. The cycle demonstrates that imagination and realization can be very close indeed. The woodcut used by Dürer in his *Apocalypse* prints was now raised to the rank of great art. Its effect depends wholly on line. Dürer, an accomplished craftsman who knew how to vary line beyond anything hitherto seen, attained the utmost intensity of expression in this medium. His bold, almost reckless imagina-

Plate 52. Hans Baldung-Grien. Horseman, Death, and the Maiden. c. 1510. The Louvre, Paris

tion is given free rein in his highly individual calligraphy.

Woodcuts (but also copper engraving) made possible a dissemination of pictorial ideas hitherto unknown. For centuries the only way of reproducing either text or illustrations had been to copy them by hand. Now, to the new art of printing were added new facilities for distributing books and prints, and their combined consequences were as revolutionary at the time as any of the audiovisual inventions of our own day. Throughout the Western world, to a degree we can hardly imagine today, Dürer's prints were enthusiastically received. Raphael had acquired two examples of Dürer's work in graphics even before the Venetian edition of 1515. At San Marco in Venice his woodcuts were used as models for mosaics. In France, Spain, and the Low Countries there were innumerable copies and imitations of the *Apocalypse*. At Mount Athos it persuaded the monks to modify their rigid conventions of drawing, and in the seventeenth century the influence of the woodcuts was not yet exhausted, as witness certain frescoes by a Russian painter in Yaroslavl.

Dürer's imagery and interest in technical innovations were alike well within the northern tradition, his first acquaintance with which he made as apprentice to a goldsmith. His two journeys to Italy enriched his vision, but did not change it profoundly. In Venice, where he stayed in 1495–96 and again in 1505–6, a great deal impressed him: the southern color and fiery temperament, everyday life, and the excesses of people of fashion. However, what Dürer especially acquired in Italy was the view of art as a branch of knowledge, something deserving of philosophical respect. From Venice he went to Bologna, as he wrote, "for the sake of the secret perspective which someone will teach me." The *Self-Portrait* reproduced here (pl. 51) would not have been possible without his stay in Italy. Of the Italian masters who influenced him we shall only mention Leonardo, Bellini, Pollaiuolo, Mantegna, and Giotto.

Back in Germany, he did not abandon his new interest in philosophy and natural science. Settled in Nuremberg once more, Dürer began to study mathematics and ancient languages, and became a member of the Humanist circle around Willibald Pirckheimer. He also studied books on proportion and military defense.

An integral part of the European tradition, Dürer's imagery was fed from many sources: invention and vision, a keen intelligence and a fresh sensibility, strong feelings and hard work, the minutiae of life in Nuremberg and all that was going on in the greater world. It is hardly surprising, then, that his prophetic art so profoundly influenced his contemporaries, nor that several of his pupils went on to become noteworthy artists in their own right.

There were three generations of such pupils. The first included Hans Baldung-Grien, Hans von Kulmbach, and Hans Schäufelein, the second Hans Springinklee, Wolf Traut, and Erhard Schön, the third the Beham brothers and Georg Pencz. Just what each of these generations owed to Dürer is very hard to determine unless one is content with mere statistics. Conditions in Germany around the year 1500 were much too unsettled to make possible the application of reliable criteria even to Dürer—still less to his pupils, living as they did at the very beginning of a new era, a historical crossroads where Middle Ages, Renaissance, Humanism, Reformation, and the beginnings of modern science and technology all met and collided. Which of these historical phenomena is to be taken as more crucial than another, the only right standard of critical evaluation?

Judging by the extant records, including accounts by Dürer's contemporaries as well as his own writings, relations in the Nuremberg workshop (documented from 1502 on) were on two levels: one personal and friendly, the other artistic. Next to copying good pictures, one basic form of the teacher–pupil relation was conversation in the shop. As Dürer put it: "It is most useful for apprentices to look carefully at good pictures by famous masters, and copy them over and over, and hear them talk about their works."

What friendly relations obtained in Dürer's workshop and printing house is best illustrated by his association with Hans Baldung-Grien, which lasted a lifetime. The influence of this friendship is most evident in the latter's work, yet it is obvious from the beautiful *Horseman, Death, and the Maiden* in the Louvre (pl. 52) that even at so early a stage Baldung-Grien had found his own idiom. He used bright colors more effectively than Dürer. In Baldung-Grien's work the colors are suffused with light; his masterly use of aerial perspective brings the dramatic action disquietingly close to the viewer. The color relations are surprisingly simple: red horseman, paler red dress of the maiden being carried off by Death—such elementary combinations were achieved by Dürer only in his mature style.

Dürer's most important pupil was certainly Hans von Kulmbach. He was twenty years old when he entered the workshop of his twenty-seven-year-old teacher. Though less original than Baldung-Grien, Kulmbach held his contemporaries spellbound at an early date by subtly graduated colors in a time and place which frowned on sumptuary display. Kulmbach reflects not just the influence of Dürer and that of the Danubian masters, but also that of the Italians. Actually, from this period onward, Italian influences are present everywhere in the art of northern Europe.

The overwhelming majority of subjects treated in German painting of Dürer's period are taken from the New Testament or from lives of the saints. Portraits and scenes from everyday life are far less frequent. Mythological scenes are still rarer, episodes from the Old Testament extremely rare.

Plate 53. Matthias Grünewald. The Resurrection, from the Isenheim Altarpiece. c. 1510–15.
Musée Unterlinden, Colmar

When painting portraits, the artists treat each model as something unique, a nonrecurrent discovery, accentuating individual features without idealizing them. Around 1500 the visible world of everyday experience began to supplant the imaginary world of religion, and so it is not surprising that next to altarpieces, portraits of historical persons became one of the most frequently treated subjects. The faces represented are those of a generation humbly resigned to its fate. Most often in three-quarter or frontal view, rarely in profile, the faces are serious, frequently anxious or sorrowful, shown in pitiless close-up. Female ugliness is not glossed over. The settings in which the austerely delineated figures appear lack the resonance and breadth of Italian interiors. The figures are usually shown half-length, with their hands just visible near the edge of the picture (see pl. 51). The hands are most often joined as in prayer, only occasionally adorned with rings, betraying a remnant of personal vanity. The clothes are still less extravagant. These portraits do not probe the deeper layers of the soul, they disclose the predicament of men caught up in events beyond their control. The eyes are not veiled or shadowed, as is often the case in Italian art (see pl. 32).

Dürer's generation seems to have shunned daylight. The light in their paintings is often dull, diffuse, barely strong enough to provide a vehicle for color. It is used with good effect in pictures that transport us into fantastic regions, into unreal worlds from which light is absent.

MATTHIAS GRÜNEWALD

Under the circumstances, color hardly stands out in early German painting. In a period obsessed by the magic of line, this is as we should expect. We are surprised, then, when we come across even one exception to the rule, an artist who is a veritable magician of color, in whose paintings the reds within a firmly outlined area do not serve merely to fill it, but suddenly become luminous in interaction with the colors in other areas. Moreover, he is capable now and then of using color for purely expressive purposes. The name of this paradoxically colorful artist in a "colorless" period is Matthias Grünewald.

Grünewald (1470–1528) worked for the archbishops of Mainz (Ulrich von Gemmingen and Cardinal Albrecht von Brandenburg) from 1511 on. In 1527 he was called to Halle in connection with the installation of a municipal water system there. Grünewald treated Christian subjects in bold compositions of light and color, among them *The Birth of Christ; The Passion; The Resurrection* (pl. 53); a *Concert of Angels;* and a *Temptation of Saint Anthony.* His most famous work, the *Isenheim Altarpiece,* was painted between about 1510 and 1515.

Grünewald gave us four versions of the Crucifixion. Today they are in Basel (part of a small altarpiece intended for domestic use), Colmar (the central theme of the *Isenheim Altarpiece*), Washington, D.C. (a small devotional picture), and Karlsruhe (one large panel from an altarpiece). The earliest of them (pl. 54) has been in Basel since 1775. In this picture the Cross with the body of Christ appears slightly to right of the vertical axis. The three Marys are at Christ's feet in the left foreground, to the right are Saints John and Longinus. The figures are grouped on a raised bit of ground. A rocky cliff looms out of the right distance, and there are mountains in the left. This asymmetrical arrangement represents a bold effort to break away from tradition. The twisted body of Christ sags lifelessly on the Cross. The arms stretch out almost to the top corners of the picture as if even the frail support of the cross must snap. The corpse is slashed and bruised. The head falls forward sharply, no longer supported by the body. Above it a little tablet is attached to the Cross by a chain. The eyes are closed, the mouth slightly open. Below the Cross the figure of the Virgin stands erect, draped in black. The other two Marys have fallen to their knees, overcome with grief: one has her hands around the base of the Cross, while the other rocks forward wringing her hands and sobbing. The face of the Virgin stands out clearly, twisted with agony, her wide-open eyes red with weeping. She is speechless with sorrow. Balancing her, Saint John also stands erect, hands clasped in prayer, a single finger touching the body of Christ. Tears are running down his face. His cloak falls in elaborate folds from his shoulder. To his right, the centurion is lifting one arm, the other holding the spear close to his body. He has seen the light: *Vere filius Dei erat ille* (He was the true son of God). These words are plainly to be read behind him against the dark background. The central drama is sharply defined, but the landscape behind is indistinct, seemingly outside space and time. It is a landscape of loneliness, lit by a strange dim light. It takes so stark a background to support so dramatic a scene. Close scrutiny discovers phantasms outlined in white against the blue-black background. Demons and devils with grotesque faces are whirling through the air. At left, on one ridge of hills, two huts and a number of figures can be made out. What all this signifies has remained a mystery. Grünewald makes little effort to distinguish the textures of materials. All we can tell of his figures' clothes is whether they are new or old. Not even the metallic glint of the armor is very convincingly rendered.

Despite the grief they are plunged into, the figures are full of life. So detailed a description of this picture is justified because it is the earliest example of expressionism in art, a manner that was to survive in painting down to our own day, and to inspire some of its most original achievements.

Plate 54. Matthias Grünewald. The Crucifixion. c. 1505.
Öffentliche Kunstsammlung, Basel

Plate 55. Albrecht Altdorfer. Susanna and the Elders,
from the Saint Florian Altarpiece. 1518. Alte Pinakothek,
Munich

ALBRECHT ALTDORFER

Among Dürer's contemporaries, Albrecht Altdorfer (c. 1480–1538) deserves special mention. He is
regarded as the chief exponent of the romanticizing
Danube school. We find his name on the civic rolls
of Regensburg, where he was born, from 1505 on.
Eventually (1526) he rose to the highest rank in the
guild of municipal architects. His paintings—mostly
quite small—depict the wooded landscape along
the banks of the Danube. Among his major works
are the *Saint Florian Altarpiece* from which came
Susanna and the Elders (pl. 55) and the *Battle of
Issus* (1529).

The *Susanna* is a striking example of a type of
picture that was much in vogue during the sixteenth century: the architectural landscape. The
Old Testament theme merely supplies a pretext for
designing a fantastic building. Though highly visionary here, Altdorfer reminds us that he had
earned the rank of master builder. We saw similar
architectural fantasies in Pompeian wall paintings
(pl. 7), and we shall come across them again in the

seventeenth century, in the work of Claude Lorrain (pl. 89).

HANS HOLBEIN

Hans Holbein was born in Augsburg, about twenty-
five years after Dürer, and died in London in 1541.
From 1515 on he lived in Basel; from 1526 to
1528, and from 1532 on, he stayed in England,
where from 1536 to his death he was court painter
to Henry VIII. Holbein is the German Renaissance
painter par excellence. His astonishing craftsman-
ship is particularly evident in his portraits. His form
is perfect, and his brushwork and drawing are of
the highest order. One of his most famous works
is the portrait of his wife and two children (pl. 56).
The motif of mother and child with a second child
is reminiscent of earlier Madonna and Child compositions in which the young Saint John is also
present. There is no doubt that Holbein's family
portrait is a secularized representation of the Madonna.

Plate 56. Hans Holbein the Younger. Family Portrait (The Artist's Wife and Children). 1528–29. Öffentliche Kunst-sammlung, Basel

Mannerism

Not until our own century did art historians critically study Mannerism and see it as a link between the Renaissance and the Baroque. In the sense of a phenomenon complementary to classicism, Mannerism is the most recent term introduced to designate a specific historical style.

The Mannerist painter, sculptor, or poet does not represent things in the normal way. He prefers the artificial and overrefined to the natural. His purpose is to surprise, to stun, to dazzle. Whereas there is only one way of representing things naturally, there are thousands of unnatural ways. Mannered works were already produced in antiquity. In the middle of the sixth century B.C., a certain Lasos wrote poems in which the letter *s* does not occur. Others wrote poems in which as many consecutive words as possible began with the same letter. The emperor Caracalla's brother Geta gave banquets in which the name of every course began with the same letter. Such examples could be multiplied at will. We shall, however, content ourselves with the following quotation from Luis de Gongora (1561–1627), one of the principal witnesses of Mannerism: "To be natural—what poverty of spirit! To be clear—what poverty of ideas!"

The terms *maniera* and *manieroso* were used by sixteenth- and seventeenth-century Italian writers on art to designate an artistic tendency prominent in the sixteenth century. They contrast the irrational, non-naturalistic features of this tendency with the art of the Renaissance, which they praise as objective and orderly. In 1672 Giovanni Bellori rightly observed in his *Lives* that artists had given up studying nature, and that art had become a "*maniera,* or, shall we say, a fantastic idea based on technique and no longer on nature." Among the opinions on the subject voiced in the eighteenth century, the one of Kant (*Critique of Judgment,* 1790) is noteworthy: "An artistic product is said to show mannerism only when the exposition of the artist's idea is founded on its singularity and is not appropriate to the idea itself." In 1819 Schopenhauer was more outspoken: According to him, Mannerists "take their point of departure in an idea; they note the features that are pleasing and effective in genuine works of art, formulate them conceptually—i.e. abstractly—and proceed to imitate them with great ingenuity, either overtly or covertly." In 1865, Jacob Burckhardt also condemned Mannerism, in *Cicerone:* "After Raphael's death no composition was created in which form and content are fused into a harmonious whole." The same sentiment was echoed by Heinrich Wölfflin, who wrote in *Classical Art* (1898): "The feeling for the potentialities of a flat surface or a volume had become completely blunted." Finally, in our century a more objective evaluation of Mannerism was initiated by Alois Riegl, who wrote: "Spiritual depth was sacrificed not because the artists lacked the necessary skill but because they no longer strove to represent it."

ANDREA DEL SARTO

Andrea del Sarto (1488–1530) played an important part in the history of Florentine Mannerism. In his work he used elements borrowed from his teacher Fra Bartolomeo (1472–1517), who had assimilated the essence of the Florentine Renaissance. He was also influenced by Michelangelo, particularly in his treatment of the human figure. In Michelangelo he found the models for his restless, twisted bodies. The *figura serpentinata*—"the serpentine figure"—is the highest expression of the Mannerist image of man.

Andrea del Sarto's treatment of the Biblical subject of Abraham sacrificing Isaac (pl. 57) is an interesting example of the new style. It is instructive to compare this work with an older one based on a similarly dramatic subject: Master Bertram's *Cain Slaying Abel* (pl. 47). In the latter, the action is developed from right to left on a plane parallel to the picture surface. This seems unnatural because we are used to reading in the opposite direction in pictures as well as in books. What strikes the viewer first is the murderous weapon—and the same is true of del Sarto's painting. The knife is about to deliver the blow when Abraham hears the voice of the angel saying: "Lay not thine hand upon the lad, neither do thou any thing unto him" (Gen. 22:12). Isaac, still frightened but resigned to his fate, turns toward the left, that is, toward the viewer. Abraham, holding the knife and lifting his eyes toward the angel, turns in the opposite direction. The angel in turn is looking down toward the left, in the direction indicated by his outstretched arm. These deliberate shifts of direction which follow

Plate 57. Andrea del Sarto. The Sacrifice of Isaac. 1527–30. The Cleveland Museum of Art. The Holden Collection

Plate 58. Agnolo Bronzino. Bia de' Medici. c. 1540–42. Uffizi Gallery, Florence

one another in quick succession twist the composition into an artfully devised spiral—an example of Mannerist design. The arrangement is governed by two intersecting diagonals. One of these starts with the angel's right arm, continues with Abraham's left arm, and ends, significantly, with Isaac's tied hands. The other diagonal, beginning with the raised knife, runs along Isaac's left thigh and ends with Abraham's left leg, which is firmly placed on the ground. The lower right corner of the painting is purposely left empty, so that the viewer's eye plunges directly into depth, toward the servants with the ass and toward the city which looms in the far background. The perspective is abrupt, and the dimensions of the figures decrease very rapidly, as they did in Antonello's *Saint Sebastian* (pl. 27).

The unfinished state of this work provides a glimpse of the artist's working method. The ass was originally intended to be larger, but apparently del Sarto changed his mind in order to accentuate the gigantic proportions of the figure of Abraham, which stretches from the top to the bottom of the canvas. Such visible alterations are called *pentimenti* (literally, "signs of repentance").

AGNOLO BRONZINO

One of the leading masters of the second generation of Mannerists was Agnolo Bronzino (1503–1572). He made his name as a portraitist and as a painter of religious and allegorical subjects. His little Medici princess (pl. 58) is one of the most charming portraits of children in Western painting. This theme has a long tradition. It began in the Middle Ages with the representation of Christ as a child and was secularized during the Renaissance. Later it led to the portraits of princes and infantas by Velázquez, and eventually to the portraits of children by the Impressionists.

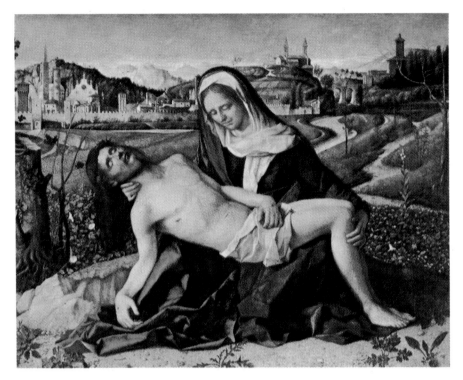

Plate 59. Giovanni Bellini. Pietà. c. 1500–1505. Galleria dell'Accademia, Venice

Venetian Painting

The history of Venetian painting begins in the Renaissance with masters like Bartolomeo Vivarini and Carlo Crivelli, who were still strongly influenced by Late Gothic art. From the outset, however, color was used with more powerful effect in Venice than anywhere else in Italy. In discussing Antonello da Messina (see pl. 27), we already noted that this Sicilian artist lived in Venice for a year between 1475 and 1476. The most famous magicians of color in Venice were Jacopo Bellini (1400–1470) and his sons Gentile (1429–1507) and Giovanni (1430–1516). Giovanni's *Pietà* (pl. 59) brings us close to the work of Mantegna (see pl. 28), who was Jacopo's son-in-law. Giovanni was the actual founder of the great Venetian school which flowered between the Renaissance and the Baroque and produced Giorgione, Titian, Tintoretto, and Veronese. With each successive master Venice gains in originality.

GIORGIONE

Giorgione, born in Castelfranco in 1477, is one of the most mysterious artists Italy ever produced. He died in Venice at an early age (in 1510), probably a victim of the plague. His early maturity and death fed the various legends surrounding his life and encouraged the production of counterfeit Giorgiones. Over the centuries, as his fame grew, the number of works attributed to him increased to such an extent that art historians find it difficult to determine which of these works are genuine, and which were painted by other Venetian artists. The relationship between Giorgione's paintings and Titian's early paintings presents another interesting problem. Both were pupils of Giovanni Bellini, and both of them were working at the same time on the frescoes (now lost) in the Fondaco dei

Plate 60. Giorgione. The Three Philosophers. c. 1506–8. Kunsthistorisches Museum, Vienna

Tedeschi, the German trading house in Venice.

One of Giorgione's most mysterious works, along with the *Tempest* in the Accademia in Venice and the *Concert champêtre* in the Louvre, is *The Three Philosophers* (pl. 60). The group of three figures near a cave, bathed in light against a landscape background, can be interpreted only with reference to the historical and spiritual situation of the social class that the picture glorifies. A reliable tradition mentions that two members of the old aristocratic Contarini family achieved high positions soon after 1500, and that one Contarini was a particularly close friend of Giorgione. Moreover, X-rays have revealed that the face of the youngest of the three men represented originally had more distinctive features, and that the oldest of them, who is holding a tablet covered with numbers and other symbols, originally had a halo. All this justifies the surmise that the youthful figure (which apparently personifies the lower or earliest stage of philosophy) is a portrait of the Contarini who commissioned the picture. The middle-aged figure in Oriental costume may represent Aristotle, and the old figure Plato, who personifies the highest stage of philosophy. This sublime work was inspired by Plato's *Republic,* thus alluding to the political philosophy of the Venetian Republic.

TITIAN

Titian Vecellio (c. 1485–1576), born at Pieve di Cadore, emancipated himself only gradually from the Giorgionesque manner. The *Noli Me Tangere* (pl. 61) is even said to have been begun by Giorgione and merely completed by Titian some time between 1511 and 1515. The group of houses on the hill (right) is strongly reminiscent of a similar group in the landscape of Giorgione's *Sleeping Venus* in Dresden.

Mary Magdalene was the first to see Christ after the Resurrection. As the story is told in the Gospel According to St. John: "She, supposing him to be the gardener, saith unto him, Sir, if thou have borne him hence, tell me where thou hast laid him, and I will take him away. ... Jesus saith unto her, Touch me not; for I am not yet ascended to my Father" (20:15,17). In Titian's painting the shroud is still attached to the shoulders of Christ, and in his left hand he is holding a gardener's tool.

The first work in Titian's inimitable style is *Sacred and Profane Love* (1514), where the figures are integrated with the landscape in an exemplary manner. Between 1518 and 1528, in works like the *Assumption* and the *Madonna of the Pesaro Family* (1526), both in the church of Santa Maria dei Frari in Venice, and the two scenes of *The Worship of Venus* in the Prado, the young master achieves

Plate 61. Titian. Noli Me Tangere. c. 1511. National Gallery, London

Plate 62. Titian. Girl with a Fruit Bowl (Lavinia). 1555. State Museums, Berlin-Dahlem

Plate 63. Sebastiano del Piombo. Portrait of a Young Roman Lady. c. 1513. State Museums, Berlin-Dahlem

originality both in composition and in coloring. Between 1530 and 1550 Titian was at the zenith of his fame, which rested mainly on his portraits. Charles V summoned him to his court. During the Augsburg Reichstag (1548) he painted the Emperor seated (Alte Pinakothek, Munich) and a second time on horseback at the battle of Mühlberg (The Prado, Madrid).

Girl with a Fruit Bowl (pl. 62) dates from 1555. In the older literature the painting is often referred to as the portrait of Titian's daughter Lavinia. It may also be the *Pomona* which the artist is known to have presented to Jacopo Strada in 1567 or 1568. It is one of a group of Venetian portraits of women which contain allegorical elements. This group includes Sebastiano del Piombo's *Portrait of a Young Roman Lady* (pl. 63). Here the fruit is perhaps an allusion to Flora. Sebastiano (1485–1549) was one of Giovanni Bellini's last pupils. He too was under the spell of Giorgione until he went to Rome, where he continued his studies and was influenced by Michelangelo. The work reproduced here was painted after 1512, that is to say, after he moved to Rome. It was formerly believed to be a portrait by Raphael of his mistress, Fornarina, but composition and colors are unmistakably Venetian.

TINTORETTO

Jacopo Robusti, called Tintoretto (1518–1594), was a direct artistic descendant of Titian. In his early period (before 1548) he was influenced by Florentine Mannerism, but he also admired Michelangelo's ideal forms. He brilliantly combined lyrical Venetian colors wih dramatic Roman drawing. Our example, *Christ before Pilate* (pl. 64), is a small part of Tintoretto's greatest work—the decoration of the Scuola di San Rocco in Venice, which occupied the artist for many years (1564–1588). The term *scuola* has a special meaning in Venice. It designates a lay confraternity (founded in the Middle Ages), organized like a guild, whose work consisted mainly in tending the sick.

Donations had made the Scuola di San Rocco wealthy, and between 1517 and 1549 a luxurious building was constructed to house it. Earlier, in 1485, the society had acquired the relics of San Rocco, the saint who devoted himself to the plague-stricken. As a result, the cult of San Rocco in Venice (which was frequently ravaged by the plague) enjoyed increased popularity.

Tintoretto decorated three rooms in the Scuola di San Rocco; the Sala dell'Albergo, the Sala Superiore, and the Sala Terrena. In the Sala dell'Albergo the ceiling is decorated with scenes from the life of San Rocco, and the walls with scenes from the

Plate 64. Tintoretto. Christ before Pilate. 1566–67. Scuola di San Rocco, Venice

Plate 65. Paolo Veronese. Moses Saved from the Nile. c. 1575. The Prado, Madrid

Plate 66. El Greco. The Cleansing of the Temple (portion). c. 1600. National Gallery, London

Passion, the four principal ones being *Christ before Pilate, Ecce Homo, Christ Bearing the Cross,* and *The Crucifixion.* The figure of Pilate washing his hands is influenced by Dürer's cycle of woodcuts known as the *Little Passion.* The composition involves many figures in an architectural setting, and dramatizes the contrast between the delicately luminous figure of Christ (white is the color of innocence) and the figures of the soldiers thronging around the platform.

The decoration of the Sala Superiore (after 1567) comprises episodes from the life of Moses, that of the Sala Terrena (after 1583) from the early life of Christ, an Assumption of the Virgin, a Maria Aegyptiaca, and a Mary Magdalene.

Scenes from the Old Testament enjoyed great popularity during that period—above all in Venice. A painting (pl. 65) by Paolo Veronese (1528–1588) who lived in that city after 1553 discloses one of the main causes of this popularity: the Bible provided a good pretext for painting Oriental costumes. Here the magic of color could be displayed in all its glory. The importance of color in painting was best characterized by Cézanne, who wrote: "This is what I call painting, this is how a painting should be experienced—as an ecstatic feast of color. You feel reborn, transported to the true world. He [Veronese] spoke the language of color. His mind absorbed things without their lines, made up entirely of colors. Then one day these things become again visible, as though suffused with a mysterious music. It's beautiful, it's alive, and at the same time transports us into another yet quite real world. ... The world has been transfigured into painting."

EL GRECO

In the work of El Greco (1541–1614) color is even more triumphant and ecstatic. The artist was a Greek born in Crete. The crucial period in his ar-tistic career falls around 1566, when he studied with Titian in Venice. It was then that his colors became highly individual. It was also in Italy that he developed the formal features of his style derived from Mannerism. All these elements appear, refined and intensified, in El Greco's later work. In 1577 he moved to Spain, settling in Toledo; the name by which we know him is Spanish for "The Greek." He became one of the leading exponents of European Mannerism.

The Cleansing of the Temple (pl. 66) is a late work, dating from about 1600. It illustrates the following passage from the Gospel According to Saint Matthew: "And Jesus went into the temple of God, and cast out all them that sold and bought in the temple, and overthrew the tables of the money changers, and the seats of them that sold doves. And said unto them, It is written, My house shall be called the house of prayer: but ye have made it a den of thieves" (21:12–13). Christ is wielding a whip. To the left the merchants are fleeing in utter confusion, to the right the disciples in various poses comment on the scene. Even in this late work the Italian influence is unmistakable.

In 1570 El Greco had spent some time in Rome where he could see Michelangelo's figures in *The Conversion of Saint Paul,* in the Capella Paolina in the Vatican, *The Last Judgment,* in the Sistine Chapel, and Raphael's *School of Athens.* These Roman reminiscences are reflected in Venetian color harmonies. As Maurice Barrès wrote in 1905, the aged El Greco's paintings convey "the abrupt, violent, almost barbaric either/or of the Spanish soul so perfectly expressed in the contrast between the prosaic Sancho Panza and the perpetually bemused Don Quixote. But the visionary has the upper hand. El Greco elongates the divine bodies. He sees them as flames which appear taller in the darkness. He surrounds all his visions with an astral light. He is the painter of the soul, the most passionate soul there is—the Spanish soul of the century of Philip II."

Plate 67. Caravaggio. Basket of Fruit. c. 1596. Pinacoteca Ambrosiana, Milan

Baroque Painting in Italy

With El Greco we have entered the century which received its most important artistic impulses from the Counter Reformation. Toward the middle of the sixteenth century a movement within the Renaissance made itself felt, which gradually paved the way for the Baroque. The relation between the two styles is in a way similar to that between the Romanesque and the Gothic. In both cases, a contemplative self-contained art gives way to a wide-open art of movement and light. This transition is most strikingly evident in Michelangelo. With the Baroque, a new mode of feeling emerges, which over almost two centuries will assert itself in all branches of art. It will also be reflected in poetry, music, and drama. Everything rational and regular gives way to unrestrained emotional expression. Religious thinking is no longer serene and contemplative, but exultant and full of pathos. Baroque art embodied the spirit of the Counter Reformation, and served as a powerful weapon in the hands of the Church threatened by Protestantism. Victorious in all Catholic countries, Baroque art linked them together for the last time in a great cultural community.

The vehement new style conquers space and plays with lights and shadows, which the restless forms engage in a perpetual duel. In the course of time, however, the originally grandiose forms become gradually smaller, more elegant, dainty. Their initial expressive force finally spends itself in the Rococo period.

The static elements of architecture, concealed as they are now under painted and sculptured decorations, are scarcely visible: nowhere is there a surface on which the eye can rest. The churches have been transformed into turbulent festive halls, which clamor for exuberant crowds. Illusionistic paintings open the ceilings into imaginary spaces, seemingly extending as far as Heaven itself.

What was the real world like at the beginning of the seventeenth century? Seen as a whole it is bewilderingly complex: there were religious wars, Henry IV reigned in France, Mary Stuart reigned in Scotland, Cervantes and Lope de Vega were writing in Spain, Philip II was struggling to retain his hold on the Low Countries, the Thirty Years' War was imminent. In the realm of painting there was El Greco in the south, and in the north the young Rubens was soon to be followed by Rembrandt, his Protestant counterpart.

CARAVAGGIO

It was against this flickering historical background that the first Italian Baroque painter of genius revolutionized Western art with his new conception of light. Caravaggio (1573–1610) was born in northern Italy. Around 1594 he went to Rome, where he soon became famous for his paintings and notorious for his angry outbursts and frequent brawls. In 1606 his uncontrollable temper led him to commit homicide, and he was forced to flee the Eternal City. In 1607 we find him in Naples, in 1608 in Malta, and in 1609 in Sicily.

Caravaggio's *Basket of Fruit* (pl. 67), one of his earliest works, dates from his Roman period. The background has probably been repainted later by another hand. This charming picture, monumental in composition and intensely naturalistic, is presumably a fragment of a much larger religious painting: this is suggested by the somewhat artificial placing of the vine leaves on the right. If, however, the work was conceived as an independent composition, it is one of the earliest Italian still lifes.

The still life first appeared in Hellenistic art. Roman and Pompeian decorations transmitted it to the Western world. Early medieval and Flemish painters incorporated still lifes in attributes and interiors.

About 1601 Caravaggio painted *The Crucifixion of Saint Peter* and *The Conversion of Saint Paul* (pl. 68) for a private chapel in the Church of Santa Maria del Popolo in Rome. In The Acts of the Apostles we read that when Saul came near Damascus, "suddenly there shined round about him a light from heaven: And he fell to the earth, and heard a voice saying unto him, Saul, Saul, why persecutest thou me?" (9:3–4). Caravaggio shows the Apostle not at the head of an army but accompanied only by his servant and horse, not falling to the ground but lying prone, raising his arms. The figure is strongly foreshortened, brought close to the viewer, and dramatically lighted from above.

CARAVAGGIO'S INFLUENCE

No painter who came after Caravaggio escaped his influence. Even the Carraci in Bologna and the group of artists around them who remained faithful to the classical ideal exhibit Caravaggesque features in their works. Among the painters who began as followers of Caravaggio but eventually developed their own style were the Pisan Orazio Gentileschi, and Carlo Saraceni, a Venetian fond of bright and varied colors.

Domenico Feti (1589–1624), too, began as a follower of Caravaggio. Probably a native of Rome, he was court painter to Duke Ferdinand Gonzaga at Mantua from 1613 to 1622. The last two years of his life he spent in Venice. His small paintings reveal the strong impact of Caravaggio, along with Roman, Venetian, and other northern influences.

Jacob's Dream (pl. 69), dating from his Mantuan period, is an imaginative and poetic work, one of the finest dream scenes ever painted. The text it illustrates is from the Book of Genesis: "And he dreameth, and behold a ladder set up on the earth, and the top of it reached to heaven: and behold the angels of God ascending and descending on it" (28:12). Feti follows this text closely, but instead of a ladder shows a golden staircase. Directly inspired by Caravaggio is the figure of the dreaming Jacob placed obliquely across the foreground and illumined by a burst of light through gathering clouds.

We have opened this chapter with one still life and we close it with another—*Still Life with Musical Instruments* (pl. 70) by Evaristo Baschenis (1617–1677). It was painted between 1650 and 1660. Baschenis was a priest as well as a painter, and spent all his life in his native Bergamo. Like the Dutch artists of the seventeenth century, he began with subjects from the world of animals and plants. He also painted fruit and shapely vessels bathed in a gentle light, but he specialized in still lifes showing string instruments and flutes, which he enlivens with fruit, colored feathers, clay figurines, musical scores, and ribbons. In this field he is unique in the history of Italian art. His works were highly appreciated by the elegant society of his day and fetched high prices. His paintings hung in most palaces and town houses in Bergamo.

The still life reproduced here shows a table with string instruments (three lutes and a violin); on the right, leaning against the table, is a cello. Left of center we see a little black chest with an open drawer from which protrudes the feathered end of a quill. In front of the chest is a notebook, and on top of it is a letter with traces of the broken red seal. Underneath the violin a bow can be seen with a ribbon tied around its nut.

The lutes look like ripe fruit, plump and golden brown in the raking light, glittering with golden reflections. The curved surfaces of the soundboards are rendered lovingly, the individual strips of wood and the grooves are clearly drawn, and the over-

Plate 68. Caravaggio. The Conversion of Saint Paul. 1601. Cerasi Chapel, Santa Maria del Popolo, Rome

Plate 69. Domenico Feti. Jacob's Dream. c. 1616. Kunsthistorisches Museum, Vienna

Plate 70. Evaristo Baschenis. Still Life with Musical Instruments. 1650–60. Accademia Carrara, Bergamo

all effect brings to mind the Cubists. The small chest in the center is the darkest area in the picture. Its rectangular shape contrasts with the swelling contours of the instruments and provides an exquisite background for the seemingly haphazard arrangement of quill, ribbon, violin scroll and pegs, delicate bridge, opened letter, and loose string ends.

The ribbon decorating the lute on the left is of an enchanting salmon pink and as soft as velvet. Its irregular folds also help set off the regular curves of the instrument, and the loosely hanging knot serves as a *contrapposto* to the rigid upstanding neck of the cello.

Plate 71. Pieter Bruegel the Elder. The Return of the Hunters (portion). 1565. Kunsthistorisches Museum, Vienna

Baroque Painting in the Low Countries and Spain

So far our survey of painting in the Low Countries has not gone beyond Pieter Bruegel the Elder. His *Tower of Babel* (see pl. 46) summed up the achievements of a long line of predecessors, beginning with Van Eyck. Light and color, landscape rendered in perspective, narrative detail—Bruegel assimilated all these elements, integrating them into a unified composition.

We resume our survey with another work by the same painter: a winter landscape (pl. 71) from the cycle of pictures illustrating the twelve months of the year. The painting, called *The Return of the Hunters,* represents the month of January. It was executed in 1565, about 150 years after the picture in the *Très Riches Heures du Duc de Berry* illustrating the month of February (see pl. 36).

The idea of a cycle of months derives from earlier sources: it goes back to the medieval calendars.

Bruegel's Vienna *January* was to influence nearly all subsequent Dutch and Flemish landscape painters in their treatment of winter scenes. (Only five of Bruegel's twelve paintings have come down to us: they can be seen in Vienna, New York, and Prague.)

Pieter Bruegel had two sons who also became painters: Pieter, known as "Hell" Bruegel, and Jan, known as "Velvet" or "Flower" Bruegel. Jan, who painted flowers and fruits, inherited his father's powers of observation (pl. 73). His technique is so refined and his rendering of minute detail so exact that one has the impression he must have used a magnifying glass. His *Bouquet in a Blue Vase* (pl.72) was painted in the closing years of the sixteenth century, about the same time as Caravaggio's *Basket of Fruit* (pl. 67). A comparison of these two paintings shows how different the art of the Low Countries remained from that of Italy.

Plate 72. Jan Bruegel. Bouquet in a Blue Vase. c. 1597. Kunsthistorisches Museum, Vienna

92

Plate 73. Pieter Bruegel the Elder. Peasant Wedding. c. 1565. Kunsthistorisches Museum, Vienna

FRANS HALS

Frans Hals (1580–1666), a slightly younger contemporary of the Bruegels, was one of the many painters who made Dutch art internationally famous in the seventeenth century. He ranks with Rembrandt and Vermeer as one of the greatest artists Holland ever produced, although there were many outstanding Dutch artists between 1580 and 1630—the period in which Holland won its independence as a nation. As had been the case in fifteenth-century Burgundy, favorable political and economic conditions greatly encouraged a flowering of the arts.

Hals studied at Haarlem under Carel van Mander, the painter and art historian. Inspired by Italian examples, Van Mander founded the Academy of Haarlem to enable his students to "draw from life." Frans Hals was especially active between 1620 and 1630, crucial years in the emancipation of painting in Holland, which saw the throwing off of medieval fetters once and for all, and the opening up of vast new perspectives. Practiced as an "art of description," painting in the seventeenth century encompassed portraiture, genre scenes, landscape, architectural views, and still life. It was

an age of mounting specialization on all of these scores. Hals excelled at portraits, both of individuals and of groups.

Whereas as late as 1545 Pietro Aretino was writing, "It is scandalous that in our day butchers and tailors are being portrayed true to life," the Dutch burghers, who had fought hard against the Spaniards to win their political, religious, and economic freedom in 1609, were delighted to leave realistic likenesses of themselves for their posterity.

In portraying his contemporaries, Hals alternated between cool detachment and marked personal interest. Like Goya after him, he gives us his sitters "warts and all." He was an intuitive painter who worked quickly, but his hand was sure. His brushwork is readily discernible, never hidden behind academic formulas. The freshness of his eye before any subject and the impromptu character of his later work have always especially fascinated; he was one Old Master who profoundly influenced the Impressionists. *Singing Boys* (pl. 74), dating from about 1627, is one of many works whose subject was taken from the everyday life of ordinary people—here, a lively, happy, merry-making crowd. He was just as adept, however, at solemn group portraits of civic dignitaries, such as

93

Plate 74. Frans Hals. Singing Boys. c. 1627. Staatliche Gemäldegalerie, Kassel

Plate 75. Rembrandt. Man with a Golden Helmet. c. 1650. State Museums, Berlin-Dahlem

the leadership of a particular guild, for instance, or the ladies' association concerned with the care of Haarlem's poor and aged.

REMBRANDT

Rembrandt Harmensz van Rijn (1606–1669), born at Leyden (he moved to Amsterdam in 1631), was nothing less than "the most original genius the Germanic world has produced," as Theodor Hetzer puts it. And besides Frans Hals, Rembrandt was the greatest of all portrait painters. Whereas Hals looked at his models much as later modern painters have done, with a view toward capturing a fugitive moment, Rembrandt's vision was more timeless and universal. Nor did he specialize only in portraits. His legacy includes not only paintings of every type—portraits, landscapes, Biblical stories, self-portraits, and historical subjects—but also etchings and drawings which are among the greatest works of their kind. Of Rembrandt's self-portraits Wilhelm Pinder wrote: "They are something that has happened only once in the world. Not only do they represent one particular branch of painting's greatest achievement, they also constitute the only full-scale pictorial autobiography in human history."

The dialogue between artist and model in the portrait—or the monologue in the self-portrait—requires a very different, more intense, more personal commitment than the composition of a scene with many figures, a detailed interior, landscape, or still life. The portrait painter has to come to grips with his model's personality, must get to know him inside out. To achieve a purely external—let alone a superficial—likeness is just a matter of technique, a quality too often overrated by people without artistic skill. What is really important—and much harder to do—is to bring out the innermost character of the person portrayed, what outlasts and survives mere transient appearances, mere physical traits. The master painter who produces such a portrait is properly said to have "breathed life" into his subject. This is why many ancient or primitive peoples have exhibited horror at the very idea of a "likeness" distinct from themselves. They mistrust it as something uncanny, the work of dangerous or malevolent spirits. One suspects, however, that there must have been wonderfully expressive portraits before such fears could be aroused—and the fact of the matter is that the Western world was rich in portraiture throughout Greco-Roman times (see pl. 8), the Renaissance (see pls. 32, 37, 51), the Mannerist (see pl. 56) and Baroque periods (see pls. 62, 63), and so on right down to our own day.

Plate 76. Rembrandt. Jacob Wrestling with the Angel. c. 1660. State Museums, Berlin-Dahlem

Plate 77. Jan Vermeer. The Artist in His Studio. 1665.
Kunsthistorisches Museum, Vienna

In the Renaissance especially, the art of portrait painting took on new meaning and acquired new techniques. Most crucial was the realization that this world "here below" is the unique stage of such human activity as ever was or will be within the conditions of space and time. During this period there was an enormous advance in anatomical study, the findings of which were frequently illustrated. Portrayal of the human face freed itself from stereotyped conventions in Italy and the Low Countries during the early fifteenth century, and in Germany toward the end of the same century. The face now could stand for a mirror of the inner man, especially as the rest of the body remained concealed for a long time in garments representative of class or occupation. There were few cases where the human body could be depicted without clothing, most notably in representations of Adam and Eve. The rare combination of nudity with portraiture is to be found first in the work of Dürer, later in that of Rembrandt.

One of Rembrandt's most impressive portraits is the *Man with a Golden Helmet,* dating from about 1650 (pl. 75). The model, once thought to be the artist's brother Adriaen, is wearing a golden helmet of Renaissance workmanship and an iron collar. The same model appears in three other works of Rembrandt, and also in several paintings of the Rembrandt school.

A late work by the master, dating from about 1660, is *Jacob Wrestling with the Angel* (pl. 76). It seems clear that this painting is cut down from a larger work, but it is not known when or by whom this was done. It illustrates the following text from Genesis: "And Jacob was left alone; and there wrestled a man with him until the breaking of the day" (Gen. 32:24). The subject had been a favorite since the early Middle Ages. The "man wrestling" is always represented as an angel, to suggest that it was a supernatural power against which Jacob was struggling in vain. Rembrandt did not content himself with a depiction of physical struggle. He also depicts Jacob's bafflement in his predicament, gripped so firmly by a mysterious power, and the angel's superior understanding, his gentle, almost loving grasp of his opponent. Rembrandt's interpretation of the Biblical text is the greatest we have, especially impressive for its simplicity and straightforwardness. We shall come back to this point in discussing the treatment by Delacroix (pl. 103).

VERMEER VAN DELFT

Frans Hals in Haarlem, Rembrandt in Amsterdam, Jan Vermeer (1632–1675) in Delft: these are the greatest of a century rich in artistic talent, which

Plate 78. Pieter de Hooch. Courtyard of a Country House. c. 1665. Rijksmuseum, Amsterdam

Plate 79. Gerard Terborch. The Concert. c. 1675. State Museums, Berlin-Dahlem

the Dutch call their golden age. As Wilhelm Hausenstein wrote of Vermeer: "He raised Dutch art to the level of the classic." This applies not only to his portraits and his famous views of Delft, but above all to his incomparable interiors. Most of these show a simply furnished room with the figure of a woman performing some everyday task (pouring milk, reading a letter, weighing gold, making lace); sometimes there is more than one figure (a matchmaker with a young woman, a music lesson, a gentleman and lady at the harpsichord). Vermeer's female models are mostly young, whether they represent Diana and her attendants, Mary and Martha listening to Christ, a laughing girl with a soldier, or women drinking wine. The male figures frequently have their backs to the viewer.

The Artist in His Studio (pl. 77), dating from 1665, is one of Vermeer's greatest works, and in a way sums up the world he evokes. The artist is seen from behind, about to paint a young girl costumed to personify *Fama,* fame. The objects shown here are the attributes of the art of painting: the sketchbook, the plaster cast, the book (perhaps a treatise on painting), materials for draping. Even the map of Holland on the wall plays a part in the allegory: Painting—Fame—Holland. This credo is stated unobtrusively, discreetly—its persuasive eloquence derives solely from Vermeer's inimitable light, whose crystalline radiance suffuses all his works.

THE DUTCH "LITTLE MASTERS"

In the seventeenth century, members of the middle class gradually became the leading patrons of the arts. The Protestant churches of Holland had no use for altarpieces. Painters were commissioned to decorate private houses, and these were now raised to the rank of objects worthy of depiction in art (pl. 78). Pieter de Hooch (1629–1683), like Vermeer, painted quiet domestic scenes. In his pleasing views of houses and interiors the figures are clearly related to their surroundings. His treatment of atmospheric space has been widely imitated.

Another talented painter of interiors was Gerard Terborch (1617–1681) of Zwolle, although he also specialized in other subjects. In 1635 he visited England and Germany. He was at Münster in 1648 when the treaty recognizing the independence of Holland was signed. Terborch commemorated the event by painting a group portrait of the assembled diplomats. After trips to Italy, Spain, and France he was active at Deventer, took out citizenship there in 1655, and later served on the municipal council. *The Concert* (pl. 79) is an exquisite sample of Terborch's style of painting. His careful rendering of textures testifies to a highly developed feeling for picturesque detail.

Biblical history, too, was treated in a new way by painters who worked for the Dutch middle

Plate 80. Jacob van Ruisdael. The Windmill at Wijk. c. 1675. Rijksmuseum, Amsterdam

class. They brought new psychological depth and inwardness to the traditional themes. The protagonists are not idealized figures as in the paintings of the southern Flemish provinces, such as those by Rubens, but typical Dutch burghers. Rembrandt's Biblical paintings, especially, reflect the life of his period and at the same time raise it to a universal level. The artists faithfully rendered such familiar sights as houses, yards, streets, markets, canals, and churches. (The highly talented Witte, best known for his church interiors, specialized in architectural views.) They also discovered the world outside the city gates.

Jacob van Ruisdael (c. 1629–1682) painted rivers and canals running through flat Dutch landscapes. Windmills provided vertical contrasts (pl. 80). Paulus Potter specialized in pictures of grazing cattle. Meindert Hobbema celebrated infinite expanses of sky, sometimes overcast, sometimes filled with the magic of cheerful clouds, extending above the horizon of his wooded landscapes. Others, Jan van de Capelle, for example, painted brilliantly lit seascapes with jagged coast lines— land and water linked by the blue sky above them. Often the open sea was painted, either with big waves whipped up by a storm or almost unrippled, catching the rays of the setting sun. Ships were painted by artists who were obviously familiar with them, for these are expertly rendered. They

served as allegories of human frailty and at the same time as proud symbols of a nation then carrying on a world-wide trade, the leading sea power in Europe. Willem van de Velde was the finest painter of dramatic, stormy seascapes.

PETER PAUL RUBENS

In contrast with the Protestant provinces (present-day Holland), the Catholic south (present-day Belgium) remained under the influence of the vivid dramatic art of the Italian Baroque. While Rembrandt and his Dutch contemporaries celebrated life as they saw it, whether in portraits, landscapes, or genre scenes, Rubens, Jordaens, and Van Dyck (the three greatest Flemish painters of the period) drew directly on Mediterranean sources. The brilliant, sensuous colors used by these painters express an intoxication remote from the sobriety of the northern Low Countries. Antwerp and Brussels were closer to Venice and Mantua in this period than to Haarlem and Amsterdam.

When he got back from a short visit to Spain, the young Peter Paul Rubens (1577–1640) was already regarded as the leading Flemish master. Art historians have often compared him with Rembrandt, his contemporary. These two great

Plate 81. Peter Paul Rubens. The Toilet of Venus. c. 1614.
Collection Prince Liechtenstein, Vaduz

artists had very different personalities. Rembrandt, thirty years younger than Rubens, was born into a lower middle-class family, and he never went beyond the borders of his native country. Rubens was the son of a high-ranking official, and was himself destined for a similar career. After completing his training as an artist he visited many European countries. In 1622, 1623, and 1625 he stayed in Paris, where he created his most famous work, the cycle of twenty-one paintings commissioned by Marie de Médicis. Between 1628 and 1630 he was in England and later in Spain on diplomatic missions.

Rembrandt's outward appearance was not prepossessing ("his character was awkward," according to Wilhelm Bode), and he lived only for his art, his family, and his friends. The young Rubens had a striking appearance, charmed everyone he met by his courteous manners, and spoke several languages. He was a favorite at many courts. Whereas Rembrandt was tormented by money troubles and died a lonely man in the Jewish quarter of Amsterdam, Rubens was awarded the highest honors and amassed a princely fortune.

Radiant earthly happiness and the luck that seems never to have left him found expression in Rubens' art. It is an art as universal as it is overwhelming, as vivid in his portraits and historical scenes, as surprising by the richness and variety of his inventions, as it is intoxicating by the luminous pageantry of his colors.

Here we must content ourselves with only two examples chosen from the vast number of Rubens' works. *The Toilet of Venus* (pl. 81), painted about 1614, shows the artist already in full possession of his powers. Nude, Venus is sitting on a red carpet, her back turned to the viewer, her face visible in the mirror which a cupid is holding for her. The image of her face glows like a jewel in a precious setting. A Negro servant is arranging her golden hair, which falls in soft waves and provides a contrast to the dark body in the background. Many Venetian reminiscences are incorporated and reformulated in this painting, and Italian motifs in fact are echoed throughout Rubens' work. Very typical is the treatment of the back, its opulent fullness and soft volumes. The bright pellucid coloring removes all heaviness from the body, which radiates a divine yet physical splendor, and is one of the most beautiful incarnations of Rubens' full-blooded happy art, which Jacob Burckhardt praised so enthusiastically.

While the *Venus* pays homage to female beauty, *The Judgment of Solomon* (pl. 82) strikes a dramatic note. The subject had often been treated by artists from the Carolingian era onward. It is worth recalling the story in a few words. Two women living alone in the same house gave birth

Plate 82. Peter Paul Rubens. The Judgment of Solomon. 1618–19. Staatens Museum for Kunst, Copenhagen

to two children at about the same time. One of the children died, and its mother entered the other woman's room at night and took her child while she was asleep, leaving her own dead child. In the morning the other woman discovered the substitution. The two women asked Solomon to decide which of them was in the right. Solomon called for a sword and ordered that the living child be divided into two, one half given to each woman. This is the moment Rubens has chosen to illustrate: "Then spake the woman whose the living child was unto the king, for her bowels yearned upon her son, and she said, O my lord, give her the living child, and in no wise slay it. But the other said, Let it be neither mine nor thine, but divide it. Then the king answered and said, Give her the living child, and in no wise slay it: she is the mother thereof" (1 Kings 3:27).

Rubens brings a wealth of dramatic devices to bear in depicting the wisdom of Solomon. Behind the twisted Baroque columns of the royal palace is one straight-edged pillar, the perpendicular edge of which lies along the path the poised sword is

threatening to take. Note also that the only full-length figure shown frontally is the shocking one of the executioner waiting for the king's nod, whereas one of the mothers has her back to the viewer and the other stands at the very edge of the picture.

Besides Rubens, there were several other Flemish artists who developed highly individual styles. Anthony van Dyck (1599–1641) worked in Rubens' studio for a time from 1616 on, but from apprentice and collaborator went on to become an artist in his own right. From 1620 to 1621 he lived in England, and in 1622 visited Genoa, Rome, Florence, Venice, and Palermo. In 1632, after five productive years in Antwerp, he was appointed court painter to Charles I of England. Next to the rich expansiveness of Rubens' art, the paintings of Van Dyck appear cool and detached—features that endow his work with a certain courtly nobility and dignity.

Although Jordaens (1593–1678) never went to Italy, he absorbed the influence of Caravaggio, who had also left his mark on early works by Van

Plate 83. Bartolomé Esteban Murillo. Joseph and His Brothers. 1660–70. The Wallace Collection, London

Dyck. In his youth Jordaens was formed by Rubens and by Adriaen Brouwer (1605–1638), a genre painter of peasant life. Jordaens followed Brouwer in his scenes of lusty merry-making among the Flemish peasantry.

MURILLO AND VELÁZQUEZ

Jordaens had much in common with his contemporary Bartolomé Esteban Murillo (1618–1682), a native of Seville and the most popular artist of the Baroque era in the Iberian peninsula. Murillo liked to paint little genre scenes of urchins selling fruit or begging for alms, but they also served him as models in mythological and religious paintings such as the one shown here (pl. 83), illustrating the Old Testament episode of Joseph being cast into the pit by his brothers. He painted a number of religious works, including many versions of the Virgin and Child, which in their Mediterranean purity and sweetness rival Raphael's Madonnas.

The only Spanish painter to achieve international importance in the seventeenth century, however, was Velázquez (1599–1660). Like Murillo, he was born in Seville, but he spent most of his life in Madrid, where he served as court painter, with appointments as chamberlain and master of ceremonies. His early works still exhibit Caravaggio's stark realism and sharply defined chiaroscuro, both of which found many imitators in Spain. Velázquez' first visit to Italy (1630) brought about a marked change in his style: the previously black shadows now begin to be tinged with color, and the light becomes softer. The paintings which (now in the Prado) he made for his own pleasure in the Medici Gardens in Rome are spontaneous reactions to open-air scenes, and their loosened brushwork anticipates the Impressionists to a surprising degree.

As court painter Velázquez was obliged to execute official commissions, primarily portraits of the king, the princes, and the infantas. The equestrian portrait of the little Prince Baltasar Carlos (pl. 84), dating from 1635, is an exception in

Plate 84. Diego Velázquez. Prince Baltasar Carlos on Horseback. 1635. The Prado, Madrid

Plate 85. Diego Velázquez. The Surrender of Breda. 1634–35. The Prado, Madrid

the long line of portraits showing the infantas. It is a delightful departure from more solemn equestrian portraits, showing the boy in a field marshal's uniform on a pony. Velázquez' figures of children are ennobled by his sublime art. Never before had the brush been wielded so effortlessly, so "Impressionistically." As in the work of his contemporary Frans Hals, Velázquez' brushstrokes remain visible. The artist also treated the little infantas with loving care, representing them not as little adults (although they wear corsets) but as real children, in a manner occasionally reminiscent of Bronzino (see pl. 58). During his second visit to Italy (1649–51) Velázquez painted the portrait of Pope Innocent X, showing his unpleasant, energetic features so frankly that the Pope complained of having been portrayed in "too truthful a manner."

Among Velázquez' larger works *The Surrender of Breda* (pl. 85), from between 1634 and 1635, deserves special mention. This is one of the most gripping and most convincing war pictures in the history of European art. The city of Breda in Dutch Brabant fell to the Spaniards in 1625 after a prolonged siege. The event caused a great stir at the time. Velázquez began his picture commemorating the Spanish victory nine years later, and he made use of written accounts in reconstructing the scene. He shows the deserted battlefield with its smoking fires in the background. On the left, in the foreground, is the commander of the conquered fortress with his retinue; on the right, we see the Spanish lancers led by the victorious General Spinola. The Dutch commander is handing over the keys of the city. Spinola is assuring the beleaguered garrison of free passage. *The Surrender of Breda* commemorates not just the victory of a nation but also the nobility shown by the victors to a defeated enemy. It is a fitting memorial to one of the greatest of historical painters, who in this work raises a historical event to the level of the timeless ideal.

Plate 86. Georges de la Tour. Joseph the Carpenter. c. 1645. The Louvre, Paris

Seventeenth- and Eighteenth-Century French Painting

THE SCHOOL OF FONTAINEBLEAU

The art of the French Renaissance was first and foremost a courtly art. Under Francis I and Henry II all its resources were mobilized for the decoration of the chateau of Fontainebleau. Besides Leonardo, who died in the castle of Cloux in the Loire valley in 1519, Francis I invited other Italian painters to France. They left a lasting impress. Rosso Fiorentino, Francesco Primaticcio, and Niccolo dell'Abate founded the School of Fontainebleau, which became the center of French Mannerism. The principal subjects treated by the Italian artists and their French pupils were mythological or allegorical scenes which contained more or less discreet allusions to the virtues of the monarchs, and landscapes. These works can still be seen in the richly decorated rooms and galleries of the chateau.

THE AGE OF LOUIS XIV

Under Louis XIV (1638–1715) absolute monarchy reached its highest development, Richelieu having paved the way for it ever since the reign of Louis XIII. Now France achieved all but uncontested hegemony over the whole of Europe. In the domain of art, Louis XIV's famous saying, "I am the State," meant that patronage of the arts was a royal prerogative. The arts were to serve the glorification of the monarch first, last, and foremost. In order to control them more efficiently, they were organized in Academies. To the Académie Française, founded by Richelieu in 1635, were added the Académie de Peinture, the Académie de Sculpture, and the Académie d'Architecture. The arts were subjected to the dictatorial rule of Charles Le Brun, *peintre du roy*.

Once again the decoration of a royal residence summed up the courtly splendor of the period, this time at Versailles. It was in part because of the lavish sums spent on the enlargement of this palace that when the five-year-old great-grandson of Louis XIV succeeded him in 1715 France was a ruined country. For all that, the style of Louis XIV represents one of the most magnificent achievements of European art. In conception, and as the expression of an absolute ruler's will, it is compa-

rable to the gigantic monuments of classical antiquity and the Orient. Since the days of the Egyptian Pharaohs there had been nothing like it around the shores of the Mediterranean or elsewhere in the Western world.

What was the state of painting in this age when all the arts were subject to the whims of absolute power? In Italy, as we have seen, Baroque art was flowering. *Joseph the Carpenter* (pl. 86), by Georges de la Tour (1593–1652), an artist who never painted for Louis XIV, is evidence that Caravaggio's innovations were more or less completely assimilated by many French artists. Georges de la Tour handles the Baroque light quite differently from Caravaggio. Whereas Caravaggio's *Conversion of Saint Paul* (pl. 68) receives light from a source situated outside the picture, and this light is concentrated on the prone figure, in De la Tour's work the source of light is within the picture—the candle the child Jesus is holding. Partly screened by the child's hands, the light shed by the tiny flame falls on the work Joseph is doing, rapidly decreasing in intensity as it travels to the rest of the picture. Like Caravaggio, De la Tour gives us nothing in the way of background to the figures portrayed.

The theatrical lighting is here used as a device to probe psychological depths. The painting has many symbolic allusions. Neither the face of Jesus, which seems to be illuminated from within, nor what the carpenter is doing have been singled out at random. The wooden block Joseph is working on reminds us of the Cross on which the bearer of Light will one day end his earthly life.

NICOLAS POUSSIN

The pursuit of clarity, the French drive to rationality and intelligibility, tempered Baroque exuberance, giving rise to a classicism that goes beyond the repetition of dead formulas, a classicism that asserts itself in exemplary fashion in Georges de la Tour. The same is true of his great contemporary Nicolas Poussin (1594–1665), though the latter strikes us as relatively more "Baroque." It is no accident that some art historians have set Poussin's classical "drawing" above Rubens' "color." *The Inspiration of the Poet* (pl. 87), dating

Plate 87. Nicolas Poussin. The Inspiration of the Poet. 1630–31. The Louvre, Paris

from 1630–31, is one of Poussin's most remarkable works. An unusually large work for Poussin, we probably owe its size to the man who commissioned it. A young poet—Apollo and his Muse are present—is waiting for inspiration under laurel trees on Mount Parnassus. Bemused, he is looking up into the blue sky, pen in hand, ready to translate the divine gift into a poem. This traditional theme, which goes back to antiquity (see pl. 10), was treated several times by Poussin. In the *Inspiration of Anacreon* (in Hanover) Poussin shows Apollo handing the cup of inspiration to the poet who drinks from it. In 1641 Poussin was commissioned by the King to design the title page for an edition of Vergil. In it Apollo is shown placing the laurel wreath on the poet's head. Although the Muse is missing, the work is obviously related to such "inspiration" pictures as this one.

Nicolas Poussin was also a master of dramatic action. This is evident in *The Massacre of the Innocents* (pl. 88). The composition is clear, the stage on which the action takes place is carefully blocked out (in contrast to the manner of his contemporary Rubens). The cruelty of the action and the horror and despair it arouses are strikingly depicted in the attitudes of the figures.

CLAUDE LORRAIN

Our own age is not the only one in which highly varied styles and tendencies exist side by side. That the same variety existed in other ages is demonstrated by the fact that artists as different from each other as Poussin and Claude Lorrain (1600–1682) were contemporaries. Claude's idyllic landscapes and harbor scenes (pl. 89) transport us into an earthly paradise bathed in a magic light. What one of Dostoevsky's characters says of

Plate 88. Nicolas Poussin. The Massacre of the Innocents. 1630–31. Musée Condé, Chantilly

another work by Claude Lorrain applies also to this painting of a harbor on the edge of earthly reality, for which the embarkation of Saint Ursula serves as a pretext: "Time seemed to have gone back three thousand years; blue smiling waves, isles and rocks, a view like a fairyland in the distance, a setting sun that seemed to be calling to me—there's no putting it into words. It seemed a memory of the cradle of Europe, and that thought seemed to fill my soul, too, with a love as of kinship. Here was the earthly paradise of man."

Claude Lorrain treats a limited range of subjects. All his life he remained faithful to the landscape. His landscapes, inspired by recollections of Italian travels, have been defined as "ideal" or "heroic." The terms denote a class of paintings, examples of which turn up throughout the eighteenth and well into the nineteenth century.

The development of French painting between 1620 and 1720 can best be illustrated by comparing

two royal portraits. Philippe de Champaigne (1602–1674) painted his portrait of Louis XIII in 1638 (pl. 90). The king, wearing ceremonial battle dress, is being crowned by the goddess of victory. The background with the port of La Rochelle serves as a reminder—a kind of footnote—that Louis XIII laid successful siege to that town, and defeated the Huguenots there in 1628.

All the pomp and magnificence of the seventeenth century are displayed before us in the portrait of Louis XV (pl. 91) by Hyacinthe Rigaud (1659–1743). The splendor of the court ceremonial is visible in every detail, from the wig down to the lace cuffs and buckled shoes. In a portrait of Louis XIV he made in 1690 Rigaud had already utilized the same Baroque style, creating a new kind of royal portrait in which the monarch is shown as ruler by divine right. It was no longer necessary to draw attention to his courage as a soldier, since virtue is taken for granted. The reigning monarch

Plate 89. Claude Lorrain. The Embarkation of Saint Ursula. 1641. National Gallery, London

stands alone, without any retinue—the absolute summit of an invincible earthly hierarchy.

FRENCH ROCOCO

The courtly style developed under Louis XIV had imposed itself throughout Europe. The period of Louis XV (1710–1774) also created its own style, which served as a model for the rest of the Western world and has its place in the history of European art. It was during this period (in the last years of the reign) that eighteenth-century European Rococo arose. The term derives from the French word *rocaille* (rockwork), an ornamental style characterized by curved and twisted forms which, devoid of all static links and functions, produce a totally nonarchitectural effect. The eye is captivated by endless scrolls and spirals, a foamlike splashing of pleasantly turbulent jets of water.

The medium best suited to the Rococo style was interior decoration; the principal aim was to achieve a unified effect with all components: paneling and stucco decorations, paintings and tapestries, furniture and chandeliers. The degree of extravagance and the atmosphere created were governed by the purpose for which the various rooms were intended, ranging from private, inti-mate chambers to enormous, brightly lit halls. The Rococo style aimed deliberately at a "total work of art" in which painting, architecture, up-to-date interior decoration, and even music were supposed to blend into a great harmonious whole.

The best-known French painters of the period are Jean-Antoine Watteau (1684–1721), François Boucher (1703–1770), and Jean-Honoré Fragonard (1732–1806). Watteau is the greatest French painter of the eighteenth century. The scenes of carefree gallantry which made him famous are more than superficial pictures of a society that lived from day to day, flitting from pleasure to pleasure. Watteau's figures are universal images of man, and the artist sometimes hints at the frailty of human life. "An entire world of poetry and fantasy... filled his art with the elegance of a supernatural life. An enchantment, a thousand enchantments arose... from the whims of his brain, from the humors of his artistic practice, from the absolute originality of his genius. He drew magical visions, an ideal world from his imagination and raised up, beyond the frontiers of his epoch, one of those Shakespearean kingdoms, one of those passionate and luminous countries, such a paradise as Polyphile raised the cloud of his dreams." In these words the Goncourts characterized Watteau in 1867 (Edmond and Jules de Goncourt, *French XVIII Century Painters,* Phaidon, 1948).

Plate 90. Philippe de Champaigne. Louis XIII Crowned by Victory. 1638. The Louvre, Paris

Plate 91. Hyacinthe Rigaud. Louis XV. 1730. Palace, Versailles

110

Plate 92. Jean-Antoine Watteau. Gersaint's Signboard (detail). 1720. State Museums, Berlin-Dahlem

We reproduce Watteau's last work, *Gersaint's Signboard* (pl. 92). Edmé-François Gersaint, born in 1696, set himself up as an art dealer in 1718 on the Petit Pont, the southern extension of the Bridge of Notre-Dame in Paris. Although he took over the business of his father-in-law Pierre Sirois and the shop "Au Grand Monarque," he did not enjoy the proverbial beginner's luck. The same year he lost everything in a fire that broke out on the bridge.

It is generally assumed that it was to help his friend after this disaster that Watteau made this picture, to serve as a signboard for his shop. At the same time, the very considerable challenge must have appealed to the artist. Gersaint, who left us a biography of Watteau, speaks with great admiration of the picture, drawing particular attention to the short period of time (a few days, he says) in which it was painted.

It was Watteau's last great work. The same year Gersaint lost his friend: "He died in my arms on July 18, 1721, at the age of thirty-seven."

The signboard represents Gersaint's gallery. Monsieur and Madame Gersaint are seen showing mirrors, pictures, and a pagoda to a client. The packing case contains Le Brun's portrait of Louis XIV. The art dealer Julienne bought the signboard from Gersaint shortly after the artist's death, and it was still in his possession in 1744. In 1760 it was

acquired by Frederick the Great; the same year it is mentioned as one of the paintings in the Charlottenburg palace. It was later cut into two halves to suit the purposes of interior decoration.

Jean-Honoré Fragonard (1732–1806), who studied under both Chardin and François Boucher, was the leading exponent of the Louis XV style. He was Madame de Pompadour's favorite painter. His elegant and witty glimpses into the extravagantly luxurious life of the old régime are delightful. He is equally successful in his portraits, historical paintings, landscapes, and genre scenes, particularly of flirtation and amorous dalliance (pl. 93). The last supplanted historical subjects in popularity during the reign of Louis XV. "Frago," as he was called by his contemporaries, had studied drawings by Rembrandt and the Italian masters, and disclosed a special talent for impromptu sketches. It is hardly surprising, therefore, that a great number of his splendid drawings—masterpieces of improvisation—have come down to us.

Jean-Baptiste Chardin (1699–1779) became a member of the Académie Royale in 1728 as "painter of fruit and animals." He remains one of the most charming still life painters France has produced. The still life shown here (pl. 94), with the colorful pomegranates, the grapes and the porcelain coffee pot, was exhibited in the Salon of 1763, where it was greatly admired by Diderot. "What a

111

Plate 93. Jean-Honoré Fragonard. The See-Saw. Petit Palais, Paris

Plate 94. Jean-Baptiste-Siméon Chardin. Still Life. 1763. The Louvre, Paris

painter, what colors," he wrote. "This is nature herself: the objects seem to step out of the canvas, they are so true to life that the eye is deceived. When I look at the work of other painters, I feel the need for another pair of eyes, but with Chardin I only need the eyes given me by nature, though I must use them well. . . . I am told that Greuze [the most important genre painter of the time] went away with a deep sigh after seeing Chardin's pictures here in the Salon. Such praise is more succinct and counts for more than mine."

THE BEGINNINGS OF ART CRITICISM

Diderot's *Salons* are accounts of exhibitions not written for newspapers, but for a limited number of subscribers, most of whom lived abroad (Goethe was one of them), who wanted to be informed about events in Paris.

The idea of organizing annual Salons, exhibitions of works by members of the Academy, was conceived in 1663. The first Salon was held in the Grande Galerie of the Louvre in 1667. In Diderot's day, about four hundred works, including three hundred paintings, were exhibited every year for a period of twenty days, to keep the public informed about the latest developments. Since only members of the Academy were admitted to the Salon, other artists had to content themselves with open-air exhibitions on the Place Dauphine, organized on the occasion of an annual fair.

The long series of artists' lives, written since classical times, reached a peak with Vasari, and continued to be written in other countries—France produced especially charming, unpretentious instances of the genre. All this came to an end when Diderot created a new literary form: art criticism.

Art appreciation in the eighteenth century was governed by the preconceived idea that all phenomena are to be rationally analyzed. All things are accessible to the human mind, the only reality recognized as absolute. Evaluation of paintings, however, also presupposes a highly developed taste. Only someone with so-called perfect taste, conceived of as a function of reason and feeling, was thought to be in a position to say whether a picture was pretty, or even sublime.

Diderot himself gave posterity a key to the meaning of these terms in the articles on art in the *Encyclopédie*. Here the reader gets first-hand information. Not only Diderot's articles on "Art" and "Beauty," but also those of his collaborators on "Genius," "Taste," "Idea," "Imagination," "Painting," "Sensation," "Style," "Sublime," and "Subject"—to name only a few—are indispensable for a proper understanding of eighteenth-century

Plate 95. Francisco Goya. Blindman's Buff. 1791. The Prado, Madrid

painting. Reading his own definitions of the terms enables us to examine Diderot's texts, as it were, from the inside, from the point of view of his own period. Thanks to Diderot, we have for the first time a reliable basis for studying the art and the taste of a whole period.

Eighteenth-century art disturbed Diderot: according to him it created no new types. It followed the beaten path, the artists never ventured beyond an unimaginative naturalism colored by memories of Italy.

Diderot saw that universally recognized standards had become a thing of the past—particularly after the quarrels between the partisans of Rubens and those of Poussin. The great tradition was dead. Even the earlier period of Racine, Molière, Boileau, and Bossuet had been marked by conflicts between tradition and progress, the ancient and the modern, rationalism and emotionalism—to such an extent, in fact, that they left their stamp on the style of the

period. Artists, particularly the lesser ones, toyed with traditional styles, trying not so much to restore them as to explore their potentialities. This unsettled state of affairs afforded ideal opportunities for art criticism. As was only natural, people began to ask what was the real meaning of painting, and by what standards a painter and his works were to be judged. Attempts were made to formulate new guidelines for art.

Diderot's lucid mind encompassed all the aspects of his period, though he was unaware of the historical conditions that determined its specific features. He could not account for the eclecticism of the painters who were his contemporaries. He only saw the results, not the real causes. For all that, his ideas on art mark a turning point, and his attitude toward painting is basically different from the one which had been current since the Italian Renaissance. The modern era in art and art criticism begins with Diderot.

European Painting of the Nineteenth Century

FRANCISCO GOYA

When Diderot began to publish the *Encyclopédie* in Paris, Francisco Goya (1746–1828) was a boy of five tending goats and sheep in a Spanish village and fighting off boredom by drawing pictures on walls and stones. He was to become the most prominent Spanish painter between Velázquez and Picasso, and one of the most important in Europe. The Iberian contemporary of Goethe stands alone: the great Italian and Spanish traditions had lost their vitality, and yet it was Goya who preserved the continuity of European painting and handed on the inheritance of the classical past to the modern era. Daumier, Manet, and Degas were the first to go back to his art; however, Goya did not give rise to a "school" of his own.

Religious themes, mythological subjects, landscapes, scenes from everyday life are not his chief interests. He does not interpret his surroundings, but criticizes them vigorously, at times violently. His world is anything but bright and serene. Toward the end of the carefree eighteenth century Goya rediscovered the dimension of the sinister, the fantastic, the gruesome, which had been neglected since the time of Hieronymus Bosch in the fifteenth and early sixteenth centuries. To unmask the hypocrisies of his contemporaries he used elements of the satanic or ghostly. The cruelty and terror of the *Disasters of War* and the confrontation with death in the *Tauromachia* bullfight scenes are dominant themes of his art. Most striking of all, however, are his portraits. He never shrinks from showing the dark, diabolical aspects of his models, and pitilessly exposes their weaknesses.

In his late works, Goya distorts his faces to the point of grotesqueness. As Aldous Huxley put it: "Those creatures who haunt Goya's Later Works are inexpressibly horrible, with the horror of mindlessness and animality and spiritual darkness. And above the lower depths where they obscenely pullulate is a world of bad priests and lustful friars, of fascinating women whose love is a 'dream of lies and inconsistency,' of fatuous nobles and, at the top of the social pyramid, a royal family of half-wits, sadists, Messalinas and perjurers" (*The Complete Etchings of Goya,* Crown, 1943).

The fantastic—the leitmotiv of Goya's art—has a tradition in European art going back to the Middle Ages. Romanesque capitals, Gothic gargoyles, late medieval book illustrations, works by Martin Schongauer, Bosch, Dürer, Hans Baldung-Grien, and Albrecht Altdorfer mark important stages in the history of fantastic painting. The art of Pieter Bruegel the Elder, which Vasari described as "something fantastic, and to laugh about," leads to that of Callot, Hogarth, and Piranesi. The fantastic manifests itself in art particularly during periods of transition or crisis—that is to say, when man's ideas about the world are being shaken.

In 1791 Goya painted his *Blindman's Buff* (pl. 95), which shows a gay company of young people on the shores of a lake. The picture follows the tradition of French eighteenth-century art, and illustrates a theme frequently treated by Watteau and Fragonard. But unlike Fragonard, Goya was interested less in the game as a subject than in rendering the circular arrangement of the figures with their varied attitudes. He was fascinated by the upward and downward, backward and forward movements, and front, side, and back views of the figures. The painting is a variation of the age-old theme of the dance of the Muses, which is found in Italian Renaissance art. Earlier painters, too, were interested in the rhythmic relations of figures moving in an elliptical orbit, as may be seen in works treating both classical and religious subjects by Rogier van der Weyden (pl. 41), Piero della Francesca (pl. 26), and especially Andrea Mantegna (pl. 28).

One of Goya's last royal portraits is a full-length figure of King Ferdinand VII (pl. 96). The king came to the throne in March 1808, but two months later Napoleon forced his abdication. Goya's nightmare visions, the *Capriccios,* which were published during the last year of the eighteenth century, became a terrible reality for Spain in 1808. Murat marched into Madrid with his troops, and the disasters of war began. *The Second of May 1808* and *The Third of May 1808,* in which Goya depicted the execution by a firing squad of those who had fought for their freedom, record the horrors of these years. Not until after the war of liberation, in 1814, could the victorious Ferdinand VII return to Madrid. In the same year Goya was commissioned by the city of Santander to paint the portrait reproduced here. It shows a statue of España crowning the returning ruler with a laurel wreath (cf. pl. 90). Behind the king is a lion,

Plate 96. Francisco Goya. King Ferdinand VII. 1814. Municipal Museum of Art, Santander

Plate 97. Jacques-Louis David. The Death of Marat. 1793. Musées Royaux des Beaux-Arts, Brussels

Plate 98. Jean-Auguste-Dominique Ingres. Mademoiselle Rivière. 1805. The Louvre, Paris

the symbol of his strength, with the chains of humiliation which he has broken.

Goya's work illustrates the general upheaval that took place in the art of painting around the year 1800. In France, an entire generation of artists was affected.

The French Revolution began in 1789 with the storming of the Bastille. The Reign of Terror lasted till 1794. Napoleon ruled France from 1799 to 1815. These dates are strikingly reflected in the work of Jacques-Louis David (1748–1825) and his pupil Jean-Auguste-Dominique Ingres (1780–1867). David studied ancient art in Rome, where he lived for a number of years. In 1784 he painted *The Oath of the Horatii* (the Louvre), in which he glorified Roman civic virtue, using the classical Roman formulas as a model for the solemn republican style. In 1793, he painted *The Death of Marat* in the same spirit (pl. 97); with these works he inaugurated nineteenth-century French classicism. It was only natural that he should become court painter to Napoleon. Between 1805 and 1807 he executed the gigantic ceremonial *Le Sacre* (now in the Louvre) which depicts the coronation of the Emperor Napoleon. In 1816, after Napoleon went into exile, David emigrated to Brussels.

Plate 99. Jean-Auguste-Dominique Ingres. Joan of Arc at the Coronation of Charles VII. 1854. The Louvre, Paris

Plate 100. John Constable. The Cornfield. 1826. National Gallery, London

JEAN-AUGUSTE-DOMINIQUE INGRES

Ingres was one of the most gifted draftsmen of modern times. Working in Paris and Rome, he made a name for himself as a painter of portraits and historical scenes. His meticulous rendering of detail and his classicist detachment were greatly admired. In 1805, the twenty-five-year-old Ingres painted one of his most charming portraits, *Mademoiselle Rivière* (pl. 98), who died the same year at the age of fifteen. The qualities characteristic of Ingres' work are already apparent in this early picture—clarity of form and delicately shaded colors. The well-balanced composition is rooted in the spirit of the Renaissance. In the intimate relationship between figure and landscape it is reminiscent of Raphael, whom Ingres greatly admired—the model looks like a Raphael Madonna in worldly clothes.

Ingres painted his *Joan of Arc at the Coronation of Charles VII* (pl. 99) almost half a century later, in 1854. It shows the Maid of Domrémy in the Cathedral of Reims, attending the coronation of Charles VII—an event she had been commanded by supernatural voices to bring about. She is distinguished by a halo, in an incomparably ambivalent attitude of devotion and victorious pride. Every detail is recorded with pedantic accuracy. This work inspired a long line of histor-

ical paintings by many artists. The Romantic painters abandon classical detachment and display greater imagination and pathos in works treating mythological, heroic, and historical—even recent—events.

ROMANTICISM

Classicism disciplined the formal elements of painting. The limitations it imposed soon came to be regarded as fetters. The various tendencies which eventually led to Romanticism had in common a demand for greater freedom of imagination. The transition from Classicism to Romanticism parallels that between Renaissance and Baroque art.

In England, the term "Romantic" was first used as early as the middle of the seventeenth century, in connection with fantastic stories; in France, under the influence of Rousseau and Madame de Staël, it came to stand for the interesting and picturesque. Referring to gardens, Johann Georg Sulzer (1720–1779) wrote in his *General Theory of the Fine Arts:* "The Chinese distinguish three kinds of scenery, which they call the smiling, the frightening, and the enchanting. The last-named is of the kind we call Romantic."

Plate 101. Caspar David Friedrich. The Lone Tree. 1823. State Museums, Berlin-Dahlem

The present-day conception of Romanticism was largely developed in Germany. German Romantic painting, poetry, and music reach out to distant regions both in space and in time. Many Romantic themes go back to the Middle Ages, depicted as a mysterious fairytale world of castles, knights, bewitched princesses, and strange, fabulous creatures. Mood and atmosphere were conjured up by ruins, bridges, and woods, and the viewer was transported to a fantastic world where he could forget the troubles of his own generation. In contrast with the sober orderliness of Classicism, Romantic art stresses emotion. Landscapes serve to express certain moods: the sun setting behind a Gothic town, a man contemplating the moon, a wanderer leaving an inn at dawn, a solitary tree.

Artists and members of the upper classes began to travel. The urge to escape from the restrictions and banality of everyday life is characteristic of the Romantic generation. Delacroix, for instance, went to North Africa, where he became intoxicated with the brilliant light of the Mediterranean. The Germans were infatuated with Italy, as was also William Turner (pl. 107). This is not to say that every Romantic picture was inspired by foreign impressions: new themes were also sought at home.

Classicism and Romanticism share a general dissatisfaction with government and culture,

rooted in a sense of social injustice. The French Revolution had run its course. The century of the working class and the bourgeoisie seemed to have begun. Daumier was one of the first to satirize the new middle class, but he also portrayed the life of the poor and of those who led a shadowy existence under the bridges of Paris.

For a student of society, the nineteenth century is one of the most fascinating periods of European history. Patrons no longer came exclusively from the aristocracy, but, in steadily increasing numbers, from the middle class. It is significant that this class did not search for an individual style which could adequately express its typical qualities (the German Biedermeier style is an exception), but imitated French historical styles such as those of the eighteenth century and the Napoleonic era. The flight from bourgeois reality led artists to explore the most remote themes: it took them back to the Middle Ages in time and as far as Asia in space. Another feature was the fashionable "return to nature" movement. All this resulted in an utter chaos of tendencies and ideas, which characterizes historical paintings at the close of the nineteenth century.

The term "Biedermeier" denotes a style which was current in Germany, Austria, and Switzerland in the first half of the nineteenth century, following a period of wars and great social upheaval. It

Plate 102. Jean-Baptiste-Camille Corot. Girl Reading by a Wooded Bank. c. 1865–70. Musée des Beaux-Arts, Reims

Plate 103. Eugène Delacroix. Jacob Wrestling with the Angel (detail). 1861. Chapel of the Holy Angels, Saint-Sulpice, Paris

derives from the name of a character invented by the German humorist Ludwig Eichrodt, and embodies an essentially German type of good-natured philistinism.

Seen in retrospect, the Biedermeier style (which is related to late eighteenth-century English styles) no longer strikes us as philistine, for we have learned to admire the remarkable achievements of the middle class of the period. The more modest aspirations which were forced upon these generations by the great war were reflected in painting by a predilection for simple, lighthearted, dainty, peaceful subjects. A new awareness of humble everyday things becomes apparent both in literature and in painting—in the pictures of Moritz von Schwind, Adolph von Menzel, Carl Spitzweg, and Ferdinand Waldmüller.

LANDSCAPE PAINTING

Out of the countless artistic manifestations of the last century, let us for the moment concentrate on one—landscape painting. It is best to begin with a brief backward glance.

The earliest landscape painting in Western art appears in the guise of a formalistic shorthand, denoting the backdrop to some action, as the cave of Polyphemus on the Proto-Argive vase of the seventh century B.C. (pl. 3) or the olive tree in the Etruscan *Flute Player* (pl. 6). Similar bits of landscape can also be seen in the Ravenna mosaic (pl. 9). Not until the dawn of modern painting, with Duccio (pl. 17) and especially with Giotto, is the landscape integrated in the pictorial space, thus providing a stage for the action (pl. 18). Nevertheless, landscapes continue for generations to be hidebound by medieval conventions. The study of nature begins to make itself felt in the representation of trees and bushes or other details, for instance in Gentile's *Adoration* (pl. 21) and Castagno's *David* (pl. 25). Castagno's landscape marks an advance over Duccio's *Temptation of Christ* (pl. 17) only in so far as his youthful hero is shown in correct proportion to the landscape behind him.

With Verrocchio we find, at last, a landscape which opens into depth (on the left) and which might actually have existed (pl. 31). In the same century Konrad Witz painted the first landscape from nature (*Geneva Altarpiece,* 1444). Landscapes without human figures appear about 1500 in Dürer's watercolors, and in drawings by Hirschvogel, Altdorfer, and Wolf Huber.

Landscape painting was further enriched with the representation of atmospheric phenomena, light, and the four seasons. The seasons were first

Plate 104. Honoré Daumier. Don Quixote and Sancho Panza. c. 1866. Courtauld Collection, London

124

Plate 105. Adolf von Menzel. Planning a Trip. 1875. Folkwang Museum, Essen

depicted in the Books of Hours toward the close of the Middle Ages. The pages of these calendars are adorned with scenes portraying activities typical of the time of year, and the changing aspects of the landscape (pl. 36). The seasons as a subject in their own right are shown for the first time by Bruegel in his series of the months (pl. 71).

Like portraits, landscapes were eventually idealized. The idealized landscape appears in Italy around 1600, mainly in Rome, in the works of Annibale Garracci, Domenichino, Paul Bril, and Adam Elsheimer. The heroic landscape followed naturally: the ideal landscape demanded the kind of ideal action of which ancient mythology offered many examples. Greek and Roman gods, but also Christian heroes, populated the landscapes of Nicolas Poussin and Claude Lorrain. They are usually tiny figures, at times almost lost in the landscape for which they are really only the pretext (pl. 89).

In the Low Countries, landscape painting was characterized by a far-reaching, previously unknown differentiation: there were artists specializing in the representation of coastlines, river landscapes, wooded countrysides, winter scenes, and landscapes by moonlight. Their works include both realistic paintings with accurate topographical details and purely imaginary landscapes of great dramatic power (pl. 80).

A national school of painting, influenced by Dutch and Flemish painters, flowered in England during the eighteenth and nineteenth centuries (pl. 100). In comparison with earlier Dutch examples, the English landscapes were considered to be more "natural." John Constable (1776–1837) wrote in 1800 that for two years he had been running after pictures, receiving a second-hand impression of nature, but that he would now try to reproduce things in a pure and unaffected way. Needless to say, Constable thought of himself as a "natural" painter.

German landscape painting of the Romantic period is exemplified by the work of Caspar David Friedrich (1774–1840; see pl. 101). The spirit animating his work was perhaps best defined in 1802 by another Romantic painter, Philipp Otto Runge. His words sound almost like a manifesto: "When myriad stars shine above me in the sky and the wind rushes through space, when the thundering waves break in the night, or the sky above the woods turns rosy and the rising sun illumines this earth; when the mist rises from the valley and I throw myself on a meadow sparkling with dew, and every blade of grass, every leaf teems with life, and even the earth beneath me is alive; when all this blends together in a single harmony—then my soul is jubilant and hovers in the immeasurable space above me; then there is no high or low, no

Plate 106. Francesco Guardi. View of Venice with the Doges' Palace. c. 1770. National Gallery, London

time, no beginning or end. I hear and feel the living breath of God, who holds and carries the world, and in whom all life is contained. Here we sense the presence of the Highest—of God!"

How utterly different is the spirit of French landscape painting! Camille Corot (1796–1875) was a contemporary of the German Romantic painters. In his landscapes he does not rely on such scenic effects as old trees, Gothic ruins, or cemeteries under the snow to determine the mood, but on the expressive quality of the light. His last works (painted between 1865 and 1870) clearly foreshadow Impressionism: Corot achieves a harmonious composition by a carefully worked-out sequence of lights and shadows, where the values are rendered by countless spots of color (pl. 102).

EUGÈNE DELACROIX

Corot's landscapes are painted for their own sake, and the figures in them serve merely to indicate the proportions. In the works of his contemporary, Eugène Delacroix (1798–1863), however, the landscape intensifies and dramatizes the action (pl. 103). One of his last works, painted in a chapel of the Church of Saint-Sulpice in Paris, is *Jacob Wrestling with the Angel*. We have come across

this subject earlier, in our discussion of Rembrandt (pl. 76). The Dutch master leads the viewer close to the action, and shows clearly the expression on the faces. Delacroix places the figures of the fighting group in the upper left corner, near the semicircular edge of the field of vision. Jacob's exertions and the effortless action of the Angel are rendered as beautifully here as they are in Rembrandt's work. However, in Delacroix' picture the landscape is part of the action, and nature participates, as it were, in the fight. The mighty trees with their twisted grandiose forms symbolize the struggle.

Delacroix was considered by his contemporaries to be the Romantic painter par excellence. In 1863 Baudelaire wrote: "Flanders had Rubens, Italy Raphael and Veronese, France has Le Brun, David, and Delacroix. . . . Delacroix, the last of them, expressed in violent and fiery manner what the others had only been able to indicate imperfectly. Was it at the expense of something else, as it was in the case of the others? This is possible, but irrelevant here. What is it, then, what is this mysterious quality which Delacroix was able to express, to the glory of our century, better than any other artist? It is the invisible, the intangible, the dream, the nerves, the soul—and all this is expressed, do not forget, by no other means than outline and color, and better than it could have been expressed

126

Plate 107. William J. M. Turner. Venice. 1843. National Gallery, London

by anyone else, with masterly perfection, with the discipline of a subtle writer and the eloquence of a passionate musician. ... Delacroix is the most exciting of all artists. His works induce the viewer to think, recalling long-forgotten feelings and poetic dreams which we believed to be lost and buried in the night of the past."

HONORÉ DAUMIER

The work of Daumier (1808–1879) is partly in the Romantic tradition, partly devoted to social criticism—"One must be of one's own time," Daumier said. His satirical pictures of political and bourgeois life have made him immortal. He has the typically French feeling for colors, for their delicate or powerful qualities. His works include scenes from everyday life and satirical parables of more universal import: for instance, *Don Quixote and Sancho Panza,* Cervantes' dissimilar heroes (pl. 104).

Daumier supplied the Paris periodicals *La Caricature* (from 1831 on) and *Le Charivari* (from 1832 on) with thousands of caricatures. He became the greatest lithographer of the nineteenth century. His political etchings were directed against the misrule of the "bourgeois king" Louis Philippe, the

Constituent Assembly, and the judges and lawyers of his time. Although many of these works have lost their timeliness, his exquisitely drawn caricatures (from the Italian *caricare:* to overload, to exaggerate) will always be enjoyed.

Caricature is as old as painting itself. Examples have come down to us from antiquity. In Christian art they are mainly representations of the devil (pl. 17) and of the executioners who are subsidiary figures in the Passion. Giotto (pl. 19) and Simone Martini (pl. 20) show them as bringers of evil with grotesque profiles. Leonardo da Vinci and Hieronymus Bosch in the fifteenth century (pl. 44), and Goya in the nineteenth (pl. 96) were powerful caricaturists. Goya mixed caricature with realism even in his inimitable portraits. Daumier directly influenced Cézanne and indirectly Rouault, and thus contributed to the development of modern art.

Artists of very different temperaments and opposing tendencies, like Daumier, Millet, Puvis de Chavannes, Courbet, Daubigny, and Manet, were active in France. An equally diversified group of painters was active in Germany: Adrian Ludwig Richter and Moritz von Schwind, the illustrators of fairytales; the Biedermeier painter Carl Spitzweg; Adolf von Menzel, who portrayed life at the court of Frederick the Great and the wealthy upper class of his own day with equal accuracy (pl. 105). The latter's *Rolling Mill* (1875), celebrat-

Plate 108. Claude Monet. Impression: Sunrise. 1872. Musée Marmottan, Paris

ing factory workers, founded Realism in Germany. There were also Hans Thoma, the landscape painter from the Black Forest, and, to name a contemporary of Manet, Franz von Lenbach.

IMPRESSIONISM

The Impressionists used a technique which had its beginnings in late antiquity and can be traced in the works of Guardi (pl. 106), Velázquez (pl. 84), Frans Hals (pl. 74), Goya (pl. 96), Constable (pl. 100), Turner (pl. 107), Delacroix (pl. 103), Menzel (pl. 105), and other nineteenth-century painters.

The Impressionist revolution, which broke out in the 1870s, was in part a rebellion against stuffy academic studio painting with its unnatural light effects. The exaggerated emphasis on subject matter, typical of the official Parisian school of painting, was swept away by the advent of the brilliant Impressionist light, at least as far as great painting was concerned. In trying to capture a vision of nature (first and foremost in the sunny landscape of the Ile-de-France) by means of the most refined color gradations, the Impressionists can be said to have continued naturalism. However, the Impressionists do not seek to reproduce

the actual structure of objects, but to show them at a given moment under certain conditions of light and atmosphere.

To preserve the purity and brilliance of colors, the Impressionists did not mix them on the palette but placed them side by side on the canvas, so that the mixing of colors took place in the viewer's eye. This device was carried almost to the point of absurdity by the Neoimpressionists and Pointillists, such as Seurat and Signac. The phenomenon is similar to that of modern screen printing: the single dots are seen as coherent forms only from a certain distance. An Impressionist picture seen in close-up reveals countless seemingly unrelated color spots, and it is only at a distance that the confusion of colors begins to make sense, giving way to recognizable shapes. Thus we can say that the nonrepresentational technique of Impressionist painting already contained the seeds of abstract art.

The development which led to Impressionism can be illustrated by three examples. The *View of Venice with the Doges' Palace* (pl. 106), painted by Francesco Guardi (1712–1793), dates from about 1770. The Venetian master depicts the waterfront activity of the sailors and gondoliers, seen against a unique architectural background between the sky and the water. The façades of the buildings are bathed in light and appear to be broken up into

Plate 109. Claude Monet. The Artist's Wife Camille, Their Son, and a Nursemaid in a Garden. 1873. Collection E. Bührle, Zurich

small architectural units. The reflections in the water, above all those of the colorful figures, dissolve into fleeting impressions. The clouds seem to merge into the blue sky. This is indeed an Impressionist vision, expressed through a classical technique.

Venice (pl. 107) by William Turner (1775–1851) dates from 1843. The artist shifts the familiar façades almost to the edge of the picture, and marries water and sky in the center. The golden light fuses the elements and absorbs the architecture; only a few gondolas provide an optical support outside the sphere in which the light is dominant.

In 1872 Claude Monet (1840–1926) painted *Impression: Sunrise* (pl. 108), which gave the new movement its name (originally used as a term of ridicule). This important canvas goes even further than Turner's picture. The morning mist rising above the harbor creates a haze through which only the disk of the sun is seen as a definite shape. The reflections of the first rays appear in red patches on the gently rippling water. Turner's ships and figures were still faintly naturalistic; those of Monet make sense only as part of the over-all conception.

Similar observations can be made in relation to other subjects. In 1873 Monet painted his wife, his son, and his son's nurse in their garden at Argenteuil (pl. 109). In this painting the Impressionist

technique of separate spots of color is already systematically applied, and the figures form integral parts of the surrounding nature.

The new visual approach was obviously suitable for the representation of lively street scenes. Camille Pissarro (1830–1903) was, according to Cézanne, "the painter who came closest to nature." Pissarro painted *Boulevard Montmartre* (pl. 110) in 1897. A period of twenty-five years, in which much experience had been gathered, separates this street scene from Monet's earliest Impressionist paintings.

Let us go back to the leading master of Impressionism: Monet. Though he was born in Paris in 1840, he spent his early years at Le Havre on the Normandy coast. He thus became familiar with the element of water in his early childhood. Indeed, the seascape recurs like a leitmotiv throughout his work in infinite variations and interpretations, culminating in the late paintings of water lilies (pl. 111), which sum up the aged master's experience of light and color—no longer a wide expanse of the sea but a few square yards of a calm pond, with water lilies in flower, and between them the reflections of weeping willows.

The large canvases are glorifications of light, and above all, of water with its ever-changing colors, its inexhaustible capacity for reflecting nature as a distorted or transfigured vision. To

Plate 110. Camille Pissarro. Boulevard Montmartre. 1897. Private collection, Switzerland

Monet, this life-giving element symbolized the transient nature of all things—a quality also possessed by flowers, clouds, and frost. Georges Clemenceau, who devoted a book to his contemporary Monet, spoke of the "merry flickering of the liquid meadow." Almost all the people Monet painted were young: youth was to him symbolic of the transient nature of all things.

Like his sea and water pictures, the series depicting the Late Gothic façade of the Rouen Cathedral has become famous. Monet painted nearly fifty views of this cathedral, shown against the early morning light, in the dusty haze and heat of noon, or directly illuminated by the setting sun, with architectural forms dissolving into a thousand particles of light and shadow (pl. 112).

Impressionism not only opened new dimensions of light and color; it also took a fresh look at the world. The revolutionary nature of this vision is apparent in the seemingly haphazard choice of a bit of landscape. Another manifestation is that subjects previously considered low or otherwise unworthy were not avoided. Henri de Toulouse-Lautrec (1864–1901) discovered night clubs, variety shows, brothels, dance halls, the bars of Montmartre (pl. 113)—all the places of entertainment in Paris where people could meet in the twilight of a social no-man's land.

Similarly, Edgar Degas (1834–1927) chose

Plate 111. Claude Monet. Water Lilies (detail). c. 1920. Collection E. Bührle, Zurich

Plate 112. Claude Monet. Rouen Cathedral. 1894. Museum of Fine Arts, Boston

132

Plate 113. Henri de Toulouse-Lautrec. The Bar. 1898. Kunsthaus, Zurich

Plate 114. Edgar Degas. Two Ballerinas on the Stage. c. 1877. Courtauld Collection, London

dancers and musicians from the Paris Opéra as his models—performing artists, in other words, who were at the time still regarded as "bohemian" and slightly suspect (pl. 114). Japanese and other Oriental influences inspired Degas to a highly individual use of the limited space of the canvas. He achieved striking effects with closely juxtaposed or overlapping figures which are often made to seem as though cut off at the picture frame. Fascinated by photography (invented in 1839), he succeeded in catching split-second movement in his paintings. This "photographic" technique of vision is particularly effective in his marvelous pictures of horse racing.

Plate 115. Vincent van Gogh. Self-Portrait. c. 1887. Stedelijk Museum, Amsterdam. V. W. van Gogh Collection

Plate 116. Paul Cézanne. Mont Sainte-Victoire. 1885–87. The Phillips Collection, Washington, D.C.

The Pioneers of Modern Art

PAUL CÉZANNE

Paul Cézanne (1839–1906) belongs to the same artistic generation as Hodler and Van Gogh. He was born in the same year as Lenbach, Makart and Marées; when he began to paint, the German Romantic painters were still alive.

Finding him hard to classify, his early critics mostly just grouped him with the Impressionists. But the leading movement of the day influenced him only indirectly and superficially. Impressionism doubtless sharpened his sensitivity to color, but the Impressionist dissolution of form went against his grain.

He aimed at durable, solid form. The dark colors filled with a mystic glow he used at first soon gave way to a lighter palette. The interplay of color and geometric form took on steadily increasing impor-

tance in his work. "Treat nature in terms of the sphere, the cylinder, the cone, with everything in proper perspective," he wrote. "Once you have learned to apply this simple system to your drawing, you can do anything. To the painter, however, drawing means color. When color attains maximum intensity, form reaches its perfection. To the painter there are no lines or curves—only color contrasts. Plasticity results from the proper proportion of the colors. When they are all there, and in perfect harmony, the picture is finished."

Cézanne went beyond Impressionism with his technique of creating space through the use of geometric form. He evolved a system of pure and mixed colors, which he applied in layers on his canvas, working very slowly. This method is particularly apparent in the landscapes he made in Provence in Southern France (pl. 116).

Plate 117. Paul Gauguin. The Yellow Christ. 1889. Albright-Knox Art Gallery, Buffalo

Plate 118. Vincent van Gogh. Sunset at Arles. 1888. Kunstmuseum, Winterthur, Switzerland

Cézanne's concern with color is rooted in the characteristically luminous hues of earlier nineteenth-century painting. Géricault created astonishing apotheoses of color, and Delacroix once said: "Gray is the enemy of all painting. . . . In nature all is reflection."

Cubism was a direct development from the art of Cézanne, and many another twentieth-century tendency is proud to recognize him as an immediate ancestor.

VINCENT VAN GOGH

Two other pioneers stand at the threshold of our era—Vincent van Gogh (1853–1890) and Paul Gauguin (1848–1903). They, too, were influenced by Impressionism to begin with, but then went on to create highly individual styles. Van Gogh (pl. 115) was born in Holland, the son of a Calvinist minister. He worked for an art dealer, taught school for a brief period, and became a preacher in the coal mining district of Belgium. In 1880 he began to paint, using rather dark colors. In 1886 he went to Paris, where he saw Impressionist paintings. In 1888 he moved to the south of France, where he died. His last paintings are inner visions set down in the blazing sunshine of Pro-

vence with orgiastic intensity. Sometimes feeling that the brush was getting between himself and his work, he would squeeze yellow, red, and blue—the primary colors—straight from the tube onto the canvas. When he used a brush, his characteristic stroke curved nervously. This is the case in *Sunset at Arles* (pl. 118), painted in 1888.

PAUL GAUGUIN

That same year Paul Gauguin stayed with Van Gogh in Arles. He made his first trip to Tahiti in 1891, returned to France, and then from 1895 on settled again in Tahiti (pl. 119). He was the first modern artist to portray faraway non-European peoples and places. The firm structure of his *Yellow Christ* (pl. 117), painted in Brittany, shows that Gauguin had already outgrown Impressionism before leaving Europe. The choice of subject testifies to the beginning of a revival of religious painting, which ever since Ingres had lost ground to historical painting. The segment of reality represented seems to have been chosen at random, and so, on this score at least, the picture shows Impressionist influence. Gauguin's attempt to breathe new life into the age-old theme of the Crucifixion is particularly daring for presenting the mourning

Plate 119. Paul Gauguin. The White Horse. 1898. The Louvre, Paris

Plate 124. Pablo Picasso. Family of Acrobats with Monkey. 1905. Kunstmuseum, Göteborg

Plate 125. Henri Matisse. Girl Reading. 1906. Musée des Beaux-Arts, Grenoble.

Plate 126. Henri Matisse. Still Life with Oysters. 1940. Öffentliche Kunstsammlung, Basel

144

ers were Max Slevogt (1868–1932) and Lovis Corinth (1858–1925). Corinth's most impressive nudes are reminiscent of Rubens. They are painted with broad brushstrokes in a free and unorthodox manner. Slevogt's dynamic impressions are saturated with light and color (pl. 120).

PAINTING AFTER IMPRESSIONISM

Even in the Impressionist period there were artists who, like Van Gogh, Cézanne, and Gauguin, broke away from the current fashion, paving the way for new developments. There were also completely unorthodox painters like Henri Rousseau (1844–1910), the self-taught "naïve painter" who spent a great many years as a minor customs official (pl. 121), and Amedeo Modigliani (1884–1910), whose portraits of young women (pl. 122) were considered shocking. Pierre Bonnard (1867–1947) was another artist who went his own way. Yet their careers, and even their art, would be unthinkable had not Impressionism just blazed the trail. Bonnard's *Nude by the Fireplace* (pl. 123), representing a middle-class Venus in front of a mirror, is notably luminous and serene. Bonnard belonged to the group who called themselves "Nabis," and who preferred unified areas of color, usually surrounded by curving outlines, to Impressionist spots of color.

Early works of Pablo Picasso (b. 1881), such as *Family of Acrobats with Monkey* (pl. 124), painted in 1905, prove that he too was prompt to break away from his Impressionist beginnings—not just in one new direction, but in so many new directions as to have consistently bewildered his contemporaries.

From 1900 on we observe everywhere the disappearance of a common tradition in European art. Stylistic pluralism is its main characteristic. Artists form small groups which disintegrate after a short period—the Nabis and Fauves in France, and the Brücke, Blaue Reiter, and the Dessau Bauhaus in Germany. Common to all of them is the search for new forms and more intense, subjective expression. The goal is not "beauty," but distortion or stylization of natural forms, which—in order to achieve a unique personal statement—is usually matched by a mode of applying color that is antinaturalistic, vehement, and ecstatic.

Vincent van Gogh was probably the first to point out the "suggestive power of color." In a letter to his brother Theo, he explained what he meant by these words: "Suppose I want to paint the portrait of a friend, an artist who dreams great dreams.... He'll be fair. I want to put my love and admiration for him into the picture. To begin with, I'll paint him as he is, as faithfully as I can. But the picture is not finished yet. To finish it I am going to be an arbitrary colorist. I'll exaggerate the fairness of the hair. I'll even go so far as to use

orange tones, chromes, and pale lemon yellows. Behind the head I'll paint not the ordinary wall of a room, but the infinite, a background of the strongest blue I can find. By setting the fair luminous head against the rich blue background, I get a mysterious effect, like a star in the depths of a blue sky."

In France, an Expressionist movement was launched by the Fauves, which included Henri Matisse (pl. 125), André Derain, Maurice Vlaminck, and Georges Rouault (pl. 127)—but also Georges Braque. Rouault (1871–1958) studied the art of stained glass and used glowing intense colors throughout his life. Inspired by Expressionist ideas and religious fervor, he disregarded the natural colors of objects, and juxtaposed primary colors at their most intense, surrounding them with thick black lines reminiscent of the lead divisions in stained-glass windows.

After working in a Fauve style, Raoul Dufy (1877–1953) developed a cheerful poetic manner, rich in arabesques, which established him as the master of the decorative effect in twentieth-century French painting (pl. 128).

THE EXPRESSIONISTS

A number of artistic tendencies current during the first quarter of our century are today classified under the common heading of Expressionism. All artists—painters, poets, and musicians—strive primarily for expression. The new trend was opposed to Impressionism and Art Nouveau. The latter, with its seemingly objective forms derived from plant patterns, arose around 1900.

Exclusive emphasis on expression led unavoidably to brutalization of form. It was no accident that artists, seeking to justify the new theories, invoked folk or Negro art. Only rarely could the innermost impulses of the soul be expressed in pure landscapes. Exceptions are those by Munch, who had brought his already aggressive art to Germany as early as 1892. At that time his paintings touched off violent protests, but they also stimulated new researches.

At the beginning of the twentieth century, however, German painting looked primarily to Paris. Cézanne—whose paintings were exhibited in Berlin in 1900—and Matisse profoundly impressed German artists.

Emil Nolde discovered the expressive power of color as a metaphor for passion and the inexhaustible productive forces of nature. In his works he sought to equal the pristine purity and directness of primitive art. In the same period there grew up within Expressionism a new ecstatic and visionary religious art, which often strikes a savagely satirical note—for instance, in Nolde's *Sinner, Life of Christ,* and *Last Supper.* In 1906, Nolde joined the Brücke (Bridge) group. Karl Schmidt-

Plate 127. Georges Rouault. Head of Christ. 1935–39. Private collection, Paris

146

Plate 128. Raoul Dufy. Deauville. 1929. Öffentliche Kunstsammlung, Basel

Plate 129. Edvard Munch. Music in the Streets. 1889. Kunsthaus, Zurich

Plate 130. Ferdinand Hodler. Breithorn. 1911. Kunstmuseum, Lucerne

Rottluff wrote to Nolde at the time: "To attract all revolutionary and fermenting elements—this is the purpose of the Brücke."

The Brücke had been founded in Dresden two years earlier by three students of architecture—Ernst Ludwig Kirchner, Erich Heckel, and Karl Schmidt-Rottluff. Their works are characterized by simplified lines which have something of the energy of Late Gothic woodcuts (but also reflect the influence of recently discovered primitive art), and by explosive compositional schemes with large flat areas. The pure glowing colors, occasionally shrill, are like an echo of those used by the Fauves.

Nolde, unwilling to submit to group discipline, left the Brücke after only one year. Max Pechstein joined the group in 1906 and Otto Müller in 1910. The term "Expressionism" was used for the first time in reference to a painting by Pechstein.

The work of Ernst Ludwig Kirchner (1880–1935) is particularly powerful. When he moved from Berlin to Davos, in Switzerland, he switched from city subjects to themes inspired by the then quiet Alpine village (pl. 131). But Kirchner is first and foremost the painter of the modern city—this is the reality to which he devoted himself most passionately. The Impressionists were the first to discover the metropolis at a time when it had just begun to develop. However, to them the Paris boulevards are merely scenes of urban gaiety, and their crowds mere spots of color. Toulouse-Lautrec and Edvard Munch (pl. 129), who occasionally treated this theme, were the first to formulate it in an expressive manner. The metropolis as a central theme appeared above all in works by three artists who belonged to the younger generation of Expressionists—Kirchner, Frans Masereel, and Oskar Kokoschka (b. 1886), whose *Port of Genoa* (pl. 132), dates from 1932–33.

The city views of the twentieth century are part of an old tradition that goes back to the early Middle Ages. The autonomous city portrait, however, is—after some interesting attempts in the early seventeenth century—a creation of the eighteenth. The most important painter of city views is Bernardo Belotto, sometimes called Canaletto, whose vast output includes memorable views of Rome, Florence, Vienna, Dresden, Warsaw, and many other cities. These works accurately portray the most beautiful squares, parks, and streets with characteristic eighteenth-century leisureliness—from the window of a stagecoach, as it were. Bellotto's successor as a painter of city views was Guardi (pl. 106).

The subject of the city also turns up in the art of Paul Klee (pl. 140) and Marc Chagall (pl. 142).

During World War I, Kirchner fought as a volunteer and suffered great hardships. When he moved to Davos he was seriously ill. He remained there to the end of his life, devoting himself to an entirely new subject, the mountains, for which he created a classic formula. Common to his early big-city scenes and works from his Davos period is their passionate expressive quality. The change from city life to country solitude must have demanded great courage. His paintings gradually became less agitated. Color and form lost their previous problematic, dissonant, often provocative qualities and became simple and monumental. To him the mountains were not, as they had been for Ferdinand Hodler (1853–1918), powerful and heroic (pl. 130), but a human environment. Cows, farmhouses, and human figures remind us that people inhabit these mountains. With his Davos pictures Kirchner is the last painter of classic mountain landscapes.

Plate 131. Ernst Ludwig Kirchner. Davos in the Snow. 1921. Öffentliche Kunstsammlung, Basel

Plate 132. Oskar Kokoschka. The Port of Genoa. 1932–33. Private collection, Zurich

Plate 133. Georges Braque. Violin and Jug. 1910. Öffentliche Kunstsammlung, Basel

152

Plate 134. Umberto Boccioni. The Departure. 1911. Private collection, United States

Nonfigurative Painting

In January 1910 Wassily·Kandinsky (1866–1944) painted his first abstract watercolor and wrote *Concerning the Spiritual in Art*. Three years earlier, August Macke had written in a letter that he had assembled colors on a board without thinking of real objects. In the works produced in those years we sense an urge to bring to light unknown worlds awaiting exploration. The new dimensions take on convincing reality in Kandinsky's work: "All forms came spontaneously," he wrote. "They appeared before my eyes ready-made or took shape in the course of work, often surprising me." While the critics denounced Kandinsky's "ghastly mess of colors, stuttering lines, and colossal arrogance," Kandinsky created paintings of a new kind, to which he ascribed an expressive power equal to that of music (pl. 137). He opened infinite prospects for art.

CUBISM

Where must we look for the sources of pictorial forms unrelated to the world of objects? In the art of the preceding generations, particularly Impressionism, which no longer aimed at reproducing formal features, we occasionally find paintings that come close to abstract art (see pl. 111). Cubism marks a vital intermediary stage in the development from figurative to abstract art, a development begun by Picasso and Georges Braque (1882–1963). Picasso's group of nudes of 1907, titled *Les Demoiselles d'Avignon*, was the point of departure. The term "Cubism," like so many terms coined to designate earlier styles (Gothic, Baroque, Impressionism, and Fauvism), had at first a derogatory sense. It originated in a remark made by the art critic Louis Vauxcelles,

Plate 135. Robert Delaunay. The Window. 1912–13. Musée d'Art Moderne, Paris

Plate 136. Franz Marc. Three Horses. 1912. Collection E. Bührle, Zurich

who referred to Braque's works shown in the Salon des Indépendants of 1909 as "*bizarreries cubiques.*"

Influenced by Cézanne (see pl. 116), Picasso and Braque began in those years to construct landscapes and figures from "cubes." In the period of "analytical" Cubism (1910–12) these artists still started from a natural model, which they broke up into small facets of various shapes. Braque's still life *Violin and Jug* (pl. 133), painted in 1910, is an example of this style. The structural elements consist of fragments of geometric forms—squares, rectangles, triangles, cubes, prisms, and cones. In the period of "hermetic" Cubism, the object becomes gradually less recognizable, and in the end all but undecipherable. The movement declined from 1915 on, but its pictorial discoveries still play an important role in abstract art.

FUTURISM

The tendency to break up the visible world into optical particles also asserted itself in Italy at this time. Umberto Boccioni (1882–1916) was the leading exponent of the new style. "For Italy and hence for Europe, the name of Boccioni stands for liberation from the conception of art as art history," Herwarth Walden wrote in the obituary for the Italian painter, which appeared in 1916 in his magazine *Der Sturm.* What prompted Walden to make this statement?

In February 1909, the poet Marinetti published his *Manifesto of Futurism,* which grandiloquently proclaimed the advent of a new era: "The essential elements of our poetry will be courage, audacity, and revolt. . . . There is no beauty save in combat, no masterpiece that is not aggressive. We live in the absolute because we have already created eternal omnipresent speed. . . . We want to destroy the museums and libraries, and fight moralism, feminism, and every kind of opportunistic and

Plate 137. Wassily Kandinsky. Improvisation #35. 1914. Öffentliche Kunstsammlung, Basel

Plate 138. Wassily Kandinsky. Points in the Arc. 1927.
Private collection, Germany

profitable cowardice." Marinetti was mainly concerned with poetry, but as early as 1910 Boccioni,
Carrà, Bussolo, Balla, and Severini published their
Technical Manifesto of Futurist Painting, which
strikes a similar note.

Boccioni painted *The Departure* (pl. 134) in
1911—that is to say, one year after Braque's
Violin and Jug, and one year before Delaunay's
The Window (pl. 135) and Marc's *Three Horses*
(pl. 136). Boccioni's work is the first of a trilogy
titled *States of the Soul.* The other two works are
Those Left Behind and *Those Who Go Away.* In his
Departure a railroad station and an engine are
recognizable. What the painter really strives for,
however, is to render the sorrow of separation, the
feeling of being torn apart. Engine power, steam,
telegraph poles and signals, scattered as fragments
of memories in the picture, render not merely a
fleeting moment but a lengthy stretch of time.
(Compare this picture with pl. 42, a medieval
representation of a temporal sequence.)

Delaunay pursued similar aims in Paris. *The
Window* (pl. 135) was painted in the style Guillaume
Apollinaire called "Orphic Cubism," defining it as
"musical" Cubism. In his series of *Windows* (which
occasionally include suggestive glimpses of the
Eiffel Tower), Delaunay combined the Impressionist conception of light with abstract compositional
devices.

FROM REPRESENTATIONAL TO SYMBOLIC PAINTING

In Germany it is above all the work of Franz Marc
(1880–1916) that illustrates the gradual transformation of the natural model into abstract pictorial
formulas. Marc's early works (1902–8) set the
stage for his advance from representational to
symbolic painting. Marc, who had studied at the
Munich Academy, first painted in the nineteenth-
century tradition. After a visit to France in 1903
he broke away from academism. Subject matter
became less important, and colors more fluid. His
paintings, no longer aiming at imitation, consisted
of spots of color. During a second visit to Paris,
Marc discovered Van Gogh, and flooded his
paintings with bright light, transferring his visual
impressions onto the canvas with long brush
strokes. His themes changed concurrently with his
formal idiom. In his early work man stood at the
center of his preoccupations; now he preferred to
paint animals. "At an early date I began to feel
that the human being was ugly, and that the animal
was more beautiful, purer," Marc wrote in retrospect. From 1907 on he produced chiefly animal
pictures in which he began to explore the domain
of absolute form. *Three Horses* illustrates the point
he had reached in this development by 1912. The
animals are still recognizable as such. One year

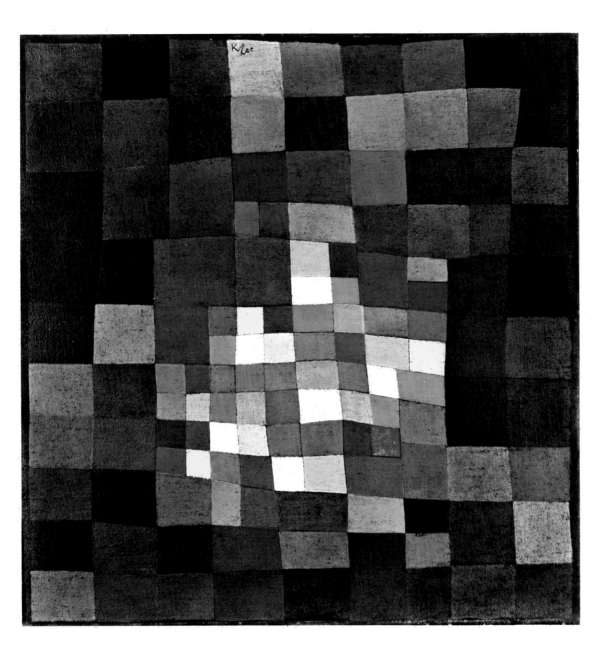

Plate 139. Paul Klee. Blossoming. 1934. Private collection, Zurich

Plate 140. Paul Klee. Castle and Sun. 1928. North Rhine–Westphalia State Collections, Düsseldorf

later they will appear as only remote recollections in his ecstatic canvases.

However, the "father of abstract painting" is Kandinsky. Although a number of other non-representational drawings and paintings were produced during the first ten years of our century, it was Kandinsky's magnificent persistence that brought victory to the abstract movement. Kandinsky was forty-five years old when he painted his first abstract work. Long before that he had been dreaming of a kind of painting that would dispense with objects. As early as 1905, he told Gabriele Münster (his pupil since 1902 and his companion for many years) how as a university student he had felt that the presence of objects disturbed him even in those of his own paintings which he regarded as successful. He yearned for an art dispensing with representational pretexts, an art aiming at composition and expressiveness achieved by color alone.

Improvisation # 35 of 1914 (pl. 137) is a pictorial invention that can be described as an example of "Abstract Expressionism." The brushwork, as sensitive as handwriting, is a seismographic record of inner vision and spiritual experiences. The work strikes one as extremely subjective in comparison with Kandinsky's later *Points in the Arc* (pl. 138). Here spontaneity is tamed, and the carefully thought-out forms are stated with the conciseness of an exemplary definition. In 1922 Kandinsky was appointed teacher at the Bauhaus in Weimar. His colleagues were Lyonel Feininger, Gerhard Marks, Johannes Itten, Georg Muche, Paul Klee, and Oskar Schlemmer.

When Kandinsky came to Weimar he found it in the midst of a revival of the primacy of the spiritual in art, which he himself had advocated in his book. In his lectures he developed a grammar of graphic elements, the relation of "point and line to plane," for instance. His paintings exhibited constructivist features.

European art in general during these years exhibited a tendency to employ elementary geometric forms, particularly in the new architecture, which was largely influenced by the Bauhaus

Plate 141. Salvador Dali. The Burning Giraffe. c. 1935. Öffentliche Kunstsammlung, Basel

Plate 142. Marc Chagall. The Flying Sleigh. 1945.
Private collection, New York

spirit. Kandinsky, too, now showed a marked preference for elementary geometric forms—triangles, squares, circles, and lines—which he painted in unmixed colors. His pictures are simple, easily grasped; the graphic elements are straight lines and circles. The well-balanced compositions hover in immaterial space, vehicles of bold color contrasts.

Paul Klee (1879–1940) developed along similar lines. His activity at the Bauhaus had a favorable effect on his art. In his *Pedagogical Sketchbook* he tells us that elementary artistic forms are living forces, organisms related to physical and cosmic laws (pls. 139, 140).

SURREALISM

The 1920s saw the birth of another important movement, Surrealism, which went on to become part of the European spiritual heritage. To get a historical grasp of Surrealism we must mention at least briefly the movement called "Dada" which preceded it. Founded in Zurich in 1916, Dada was one of many manifestations of revolt againt bourgeois convention. Stressing chance and spontaneity, it produced unusual works in collage, woodcut, and relief—a mixture of art and ironic protest,

often inspired by a desire to shock the bourgeoisie.

In 1917 a number of Dadaists moved to Berlin. The most talented among them was without doubt Georg Grosz. He savagely caricatured militarism, urban immorality, contempt for the war wounded, and, most savagely of all, war profiteers. Another artist inspired by disgust and horror in his late Expressionist paintings was Otto Dix. Like Grosz, Dix left the Dada group and developed an individual idiom not unrelated to traditional conceptions of the object. Eventually, after many false starts, he arrived at an expressive style tinged with religiosity. In Hanover, Kurt Schwitters (1887–1948) championed Dadaism in his magazine *Merz* (1923–32). In his collages he investigated the artistic value of the contents of waste baskets and other refuse.

Surrealism profited from the Dada experience, but (as André Breton wrote in his *First Manifesto of Surrealism* of 1924) it is largely based on the belief in the higher reality of certain forms of association hitherto neglected, the supreme power of dreams, and the spontaneous activity of the mind. According to Breton, Surrealism seeks to do away with all psychic mechanisms other than these as a way of solving the essential problems of life. Such statements were directed against a reliance on reason thought to be obsolete, and raised the activity of dream to the rank of thought. Sigmund

Plate 143. Marc Chagall. I and the Village. 1911. Museum of Modern Art, New York. Mrs. Simon Guggenheim Fund

Plate 144. Alfred Manessier. Night. 1956. Private collection, Oslo

Freud, but also Lautréamont, Rimbaud, Jarry, and Apollinaire, have made us aware that the conscious mind is but one tiny spill of light in the otherwise dark world of the unconscious psyche. Only in his dreams does man gain a precarious grasp of the resources he holds within himself. Surrealism seeks to give access to these hidden regions, to make them available to art and imagination. The Surrealist artist or poet surrenders himself to visions rising from his unconscious, thus becoming a passive medium for the expression of the creative power within him, which does not really belong to him. He has rightly been compared to a precision mechanic who assembles finished parts according to a blueprint he does not understand, and to whom the final result comes as a surprise. Chance is deliberately used as a factor in the process of creation.

In the *Second Manifesto of Surrealism* (1930), Breton says that the Surrealist image aims at concretizing an inner model. "Everything suggests that there is a certain point in the mind where life and death, the real and the imaginary, the past and the future, what can and what cannot be said in words are no longer perceived as opposites. The whole of Surrealist activity is motivated solely by the effort to locate this point."

The most prominent Surrealist painters are Giorgio de Chirico, Yves Tanguy, Max Ernst, Sal-

vador Dali (pl. 141), and Joan Miró. Marc Chagall (b. 1887) cannot be classified so easily. His artistic territory borders on children's paintings (pl. 143), Russian icons, nineteenth-century naturalism, Impressionism, and all the *isms* that followed. *The Flying Sleigh* (pl. 142) shown above the roof of Vitebsk (Chagall's native town in White Russia) seems to be the product of a dark night's dream.

Alfred Manessier (b. 1911) is an outstanding representative of the School of Paris, which since 1945 has included various artistic tendencies. In his *Night* (pl. 144), he starts from the visible world, reducing it to simple evocative signs and symbols. Such formulas have become accepted all over the world as a kind of visual Esperanto, and as such imply the dangers of uniformity and superficiality.

ACTION PAINTING

Modern art is no longer a European monopoly. Some of its important impulses come from the United States. One of the most talented artists of the first half of the twentieth century was Jackson Pollock (1912–1956). He spent his youth in Arizona and North Carolina, and studied in Los Angeles and New York. In 1940 he began to produce abstract paintings. His technique is unusual. He gives free rein to spontaneity. The paint, dripped or splashed on the canvas, seems to have freed itself from any restraint imposed by the picture surface. Conventional shapes give way to a vibrant, cosmic calligraphy (pl. 145).

The artist described his working method as follows: "My painting does not come from the easel. I hardly ever stretch my canvas before painting. I prefer to tack the unstretched canvas to the hard wall or floor. I need the resistance of a hard surface. On the floor I am more at ease. I feel nearer, more a part of the painting, since this way I can walk round it, work from the four sides and literally be *in* the painting. This is akin to the method of the Indian sand painters of the West.

"I continue to get further away from the usual painter's tools such as easel, palette, brushes, etc. I prefer sticks, trowels, knives and dripping fluid paint or a heavy impasto with sand, broken glass and other foreign matter added.

"When I am *in* my painting, I'm not aware of what I'm doing. It is only after a sort of 'get acquainted' period that I see what I have been about. I have no fears about making changes, destroying the image, etc., because the painting has a life of its own. I try to let it come through. It is only when I lose contact with the painting that the result is a mess. Otherwise there is pure harmony, an easy give and take, and the painting comes out well" ("My Painting," *Possibilities* I, New York, Winter 1947–48).

THE PRESENT

Historians stop short at evaluating contemporary work. What the various existing, frequently conflicting styles of painting—which originated in Europe and after the Second World War also in America—have produced requires a certain distance to be judged, classified, and appreciated.

Every kind of painting is and always has been experimental. Today a given tendency reflects a given artist's attempt to orient himself in an increasingly bewildering world, to obtain room in which his spirit can breathe and his pulse beat freely. Whatever his artistic creed, whether his art is figurative or abstract, the artist expresses the unrepresentable in representable form. He is the prophet who leads us from what is invisible today to what will be visible tomorrow.

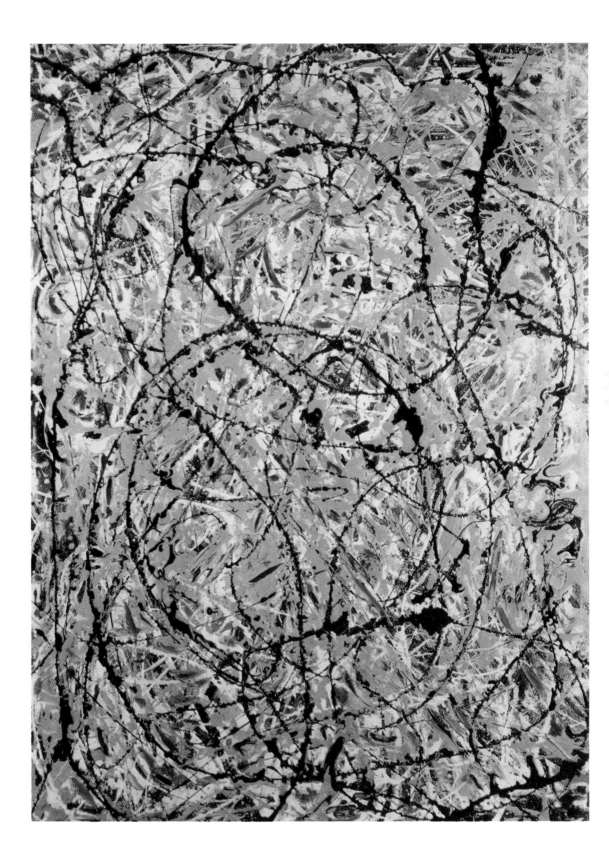

Plate 145. Jackson Pollock. Winding Paths. Galleria d'Arte Moderna, Rome

List of Plates

(references are to plate numbers)